Praise for

Until All You See Is Sky

"Like his stories, George Choundas's essays
are a winning brew of rigor, compassion,
humor, and just a touch of melancholy.
Reading them will make you
feel less alone."

–DAVID LEAVITT, author of *Shelter in Place,*
The Lost Language of Cranes, and *The Page Turner*

—

"The places of *Until All You See Is Sky* —
from the Parthenon to the Tampa outpost of
Payless Shoes and many spots in between —
build out a compelling constellation
of sites, giving dimension to the
father, son, and generous human
who anchors this essay collection.
With playful language and an unceasing
impulse to understand the world around
him, Choundas makes his readers see
the nooks and crannies of this rock of ours
(even Midtown Manhattan!) with a
new and expansive appreciation."

— EMILY NEMENS, author of *The Cactus League*

Until All You See Is Sky

George Choundas

EASTOVER
— PRESS —

Until All You See Is Sky

George Choundas

ESSAYS

ISBN 978-1-958094-04-4

BOOK & COVER DESIGN — EK Larken

EastOver Press encourages the use of our publications in
educational settings. For questions about educational discounts,
contact us online:. www.EastOverPress.com
or info@EastOverPress.com

PUBLISHED IN THE UNITED STATES OF AMERICA BY

EASTOVER
— PRESS —
ROCHESTER, MASSASSACHUSETTS
www.EastOverPress.com

Until All You See Is
Sky

Contents

Paylessness 11

Why I Write 31

I [Hard-Clenched Knuckle-Forward Fist] New York 39

The Vengeances 47

87th and Abomination 71

The Petervian Calendar 77

Dead Now 83

Tampa, Florida, 1184 B.C. 95

Glory, Finally, at the Parker House 101

Nothing Like a Pandemic 113

My Muse Is Gaffay 119

In the Covidium 125

The Middle of the Center 135

ACKNOWLEDGMENTS 183

ABOUT THE AUTHOR 185

—

Paylessness

—

OF ALL THE STREETS IN TAMPA, THE MOST NOTABLE, arguably, is Howard.

I grew up near Howard Avenue. In the 1980s, it was a longitudinal wreck. Boarded-up cigar factories and brick shells loomed every several blocks. Between and behind these teemed small and dilapidated homes, some so old they'd supposedly housed the original cigar workers. Their porches, carious and askew, resembled pensioner teeth. Many of the facades showed somewhere a patch of debrided slatting that let the sunlight have its way, that let people see — wall frame, particleboard — what they weren't supposed to see. Following existential matters of health and subsistence, maybe it's how readily strangers can see your particular squalor that makes the biggest difference between wealth and want. The rich keep fence-ringed, lawn-moated, drape-cloaked houses with rooms and rooms. You'll never see their tears and their underwear. The needy, what little they have, have even less to hide the little behind. You'll see their underwear and their tears, and more, and their sovereign resource is pretending not to mind.

Today, Howard Avenue is a prestige address. South Tampa brokers love a Howard listing like a dog loves seven bones. The street itself begins geographically at Bayshore Boulevard — a waterfront esplanade replete with mansions — and from there the luxe has spread rashwise. Erstwhile muffler shops now serve tapas. The brownfields are greenswards; the scree farms they call empty lots have bloomed condos. There are whole contrived neighborhoods known as SoHo and NoHo — for South Howard and North Howard — and I'll write the names but I won't say them aloud because in this life you play along with one little fraud and soon enough you're getting tri-married in Ibiza by a giraffe officiant. No, thank you.

This is a story about the bridging of opposite worlds. It is perhaps fitting, therefore, that Howard starts at magnificent Bayshore Boulevard in South Tampa and dead-ends in a Payless ShoeSource in West Tampa. The dead end is where Howard merges finally into its sister street, Armenia Avenue, after running parallel for a distance. Howard and Armenia, at this location, are like radius and ulna turned humerus. Were you to ignore the merge and continue along Howard's original vector while, say, daydreaming of hand-rolled cigars, you'd drive right through the front door of my childhood discount shoe store.

We moved to Tampa from the working-class, Spanish-speaking part of Weehawken, New Jersey, when I was nine. It was a weird transition for us, my parents and my sister and me. In Tampa, I attended an Episcopalian church school — on scholarship, because we had no money. Every morning one of my parents drove me southbound on Armenia to get to school, and every afternoon we took northbound Howard to get back home. The school had a few other kids from modest households, but most were the scions of South Tampa's elite. They sported last names that were also outdoor nouns: Hedges and Hillock and Barnes. Their families boarded jets in the winter to ski and in the summer to surf. (I did not know that surfing was something real people did. Thus, you may conservatively infer that I did not know that surfing the Gulf of Mexico's lazy, mounded waves was out of the question.) I still remember them trying to explain *cotillion* to me, a venture destined to fail for radical lack of foundation.

Paul has cotillion tonight.

He has what?

Cotillion.

What's that?

You know, where you learn to dance.

A ballroom?

Not really.

What word are you saying?

Cotillion.

How do you spell? [Not: How do you spell it? Just: How do you spell? In situations where I'm caught utterly ignorant of a thing, I find myself shedding involuntarily all the education and poise I've managed to accumulate in life, as if the part of my brain that feels like a caveman bullies the other parts — bullying presumably being one thing at which cavemen excelled — into not showing it up and so, for their part, talking and acting like cavemen.]

C-o-t-i-l-l-i-o-n.

A kind of dancing, this?

It's where you learn to dance. It sucks.

Why you do?

I don't do it. I quit a year ago. Paul does it. His parents make him.

His parents dance with him?

Just—it sucks.

When they weren't dancing, the parents drove gull-wing vehicles. Many of them. In fairness, I may not have seen a representative sample of their cars, given the school was a block from Bayshore and so many of the kids simply walked to their mansion homes. In seventh and eighth grades, our Physical Education classes consisted of running through the neighborhood cross-country-style. The kids observed a weird gentility by never pointing out their own houses as we passed but falling over each other to point out everybody else's. Gesturing wildly: That's where Bryce lives! That's Bryce's house! Bryce, impassive, benign, wouldn't look up at his own seven-bedroom with its wraparound porch and rotating gazebo wound twice daily by a live-in Swiss engineer. Bryce would continue striding ahead, facing forward and a little down, exhibiting as he loped the noble mien of all history's warriors with head and shoulders steadfast and eyes trained on where, if trees and buildings were transparent, the horizon would lie. Yet as soon as we passed Andra's house, here was Bryce, hopping excitedly like a toddler at his first carnival, yelping: That's where Andra lives! That's Andra's house!

Eventually, my Cuban-born mother, a reading teacher, found a job teaching English as a second language to migrant workers. She'd taught in the Bronx when we lived in Jersey, and in moving to Florida she'd traded tenure and pen-

sion in New York City schools for a part-time
position in a half-empty school across the street
from a goat pen. My Greek-born father, who'd
operated a hot dog truck in New Jersey, was
unemployed. Tampa boasted foot traffic com-
mensurate with its car culture and superheat-
ed pavements and so had little hospitality for
the street vendor. Circumstances like that, why
would we *not* have bought our shoes from Payless? We shopped there for the same reason that
everyone who shopped at Payless ShoeSource
called it simply "Payless." The shoes themselves
mattered, but not much. They had to be shoes,
first of all, and second of all, they had to look
more or less like shoes. As for "source," this
was a Veblenesque, morally decadent notion
that K-Mart–frequenting immigrant parents like
mine loved to disparage. The paylessness was
central, was everything.

By the mid-1980s, the rest of America had
abandoned the yellows and browns that so conspicuously defined the previous decade's interiors. Not Payless. The opposite: it brandished
those hues like a flag atop an encampment of re-
vanchist aesthetes. Even the interior lighting —
which by easy default should have been a clean,
expositional white — was medievally yellow,
soiling everything beneath. The sodium bulb in-
dustry owes its existence to bus terminals, loading docks, beverage wholesalers, and Payless locations. You followed that sullen intestinal glow
inside, and your face smashed directly into a
plate of stench: the reek of freshly manufactured
plastics and vinyls, so definite and unfleeting it
was like an inner set of doors you'd forgotten to

open.

The aisles at Payless were half as wide as the shelving on either side was tall. This, combined with the heady, intricate scent of synthetics, transformed each aisle into an alien passage. None of that clichéd twenty-second-century gimmickry, all metal on metal, shellacked in clinical light. Instead: yellow from above, and carpet underfoot. Indeed, one compelled the other: when light is the color of moth wings and wind-shorn bark, it needs after falling a textured surface in which to sift down and finally settle.

The day-to-day protocol at Payless was assiduously observed. Only two people worked the store at any given time. One handled the register while the other roved the floor, assisting customers and reshelving merchandise. Payless: retrograde in décor but prescient in matters of business administration, for by 1982 it had mastered the defining trend of twenty-first-century retail, other than dying off completely, which is skeletal staffing. At the Armenia location, these two never spoke English, only Spanish, and from time to time, apropos of nothing, they'd yell at the top of their lungs at each other.

¡¿Pero donde?!

¡Ya te dije!

¡No me dijiste nada!

¡Ay, Benni, por favor!

My mother was skilled at persuading me to get shoes a size too large. I'd try on a pair and protest that, essentially, I was skating back and forth across two tiny ponds. She'd point at the laces, explain gently that laces, by dint of being laces, were things that could always be pulled tighter, and wonder aloud why such a clever invention would even materialize if everybody adored the fit of their shoes the instant they put them on. I'd complain how the heels of my feet launched out of the heels of the shoes with every step. She'd suggest that I was habituated like all juveniles to the false comfort of tight shoes, an inevitable result of growth spurts outpacing shoe store visits (*Whose fault was that?* I should have said, it occurs to me now, an *esprit d'escalier* nearly four decades in the making), and that it was a matter of time before I understood like all grown men that a healthy uncramped space for the toes and arch was more important than the prospect of dominating some triviality like Capture the Flag because my second-skin shoes allowed me the sharpest turns and suddenest stops. (She didn't say "triviality," but it was richly implied.)

In short, like every accomplished immigrant, my mother scraped on both ends. On the front end, she shopped at Payless. On the back end, she gaslighted me into a size that would delay the next trip to Payless.

Her only problem was my age. Middle school was when the fashion scales fell from my eyes. In sixth and seventh grades, I marveled that my closet contained a pair of boat shoes just like the Sperry Top-Siders worn by Thomas Magnum on television's *Magnum P.I.* By eighth grade, I'd discovered that what I'd been wearing on my feet for two years was plastic. They were hoax shoes not boat shoes, extruded from a mixed melt of trickery and polypropylene. Even after I'd passed between these polar states of knowledge — from oblivious garden-grade bliss to grim wounded canniness — my mind cavorted in elaborate denial. I'd gaze at my shoes and endlessly ask myself counterfactuals like, *Would a passerby notice they were synthetic? How about someone sitting at one table of a mall food court while I sat at another? Which might be the giveaway: the way they catch the light, or the way a flexed forefoot yields a single large pleat without ancillary creasing?* In the time I spent daring myself to see my shoes for cheats, I could have singlehandedly found a cure for telomere degradation, or at least cobbled an actual pair of genuine-leather tassel loafers after raising two calves to peak bovinity and snipping off their tails. (If this is not how leather loafer tassels are made, do not act surprised I know so little about premium cordwainery, because let me be clear about this: I got my shoes at Payless.)

So cotillion is the place you go?

What do you mean?

Like, it is where Paul goes? Like a pavilion?

It's a thing you go to, like soccer practice.

Why don't they just say dance practice?

'Cause it's cotillion. 'Cause it sucks.

This story has consisted of a lot of griping. But it's a happy one, actually. It involves three felicities. The first is that just a few yards from Payless, wedged in the crotch between Armenia and Howard, was a Church's Chicken, and by God they serve fried okra at Church's Chicken, and on those occasions that found my mother both especially hungry and especially in a good mood, she'd spring for chicken and two sides.

Church's was excellent, gustatorily and psycho-
logically. It supplied a rare opportunity to look
down on other people. I'd see other customers
with mashed potatoes. I'd see fools with cole
slaw. I was the only one with a double portion
of okra — I was king, therefore, and mighty — and
I'd shake my head, daring them to ask me why I
was shaking my head. Nobody asked. But here's
what: when your scepter is delicious, you don't
need anybody to do anything.

The second felicity was the family's circumstances. By the time I hit eighth grade,
my mother had found a full-time position as a
reading resource teacher. My father was running his own sandwich shop in an office park.
Life was looking up. Wait, no. That formulation
is at once hackneyed and altogether inadequate.
Let me try it this way:

The world was smiling on our little family.
And there are certain events so happy and implausible that they are properly understood
only as congratulations for this broader tranche
of luck. They are markers that the eras in which
they occurred were large-scale blessings so that
history won't forget. In 1980, smallpox was
declared eradicated. In 1988, the Berlin Wall
came down. In 1984, I got a pair of Stan Smiths.

My mother bought the Stan Smiths for me
at Maas Brothers. Maas Brothers was then the
fanciest department store in West Shore Plaza,
which was then the fanciest mall in all of Tampa.
Tampa is mall country, and Tampanians know
malls, and so please know that saying *the fanciest
store in the fanciest mall in Tampa* is like saying
the palest of all the Russian accountants. It really

is saying something. Now, did we buy them on sale? I can't remember. So I don't know for sure, in the same way I don't know for sure whether after my next inhalation I'll necessarily exhale. I don't know everything.

A pair of Adidas Stan Smiths was a magical asset. A Flock of Seagulls concert T-shirt, say, or a pair of Ocean Pacific shorts, couldn't be worn more than once a week without inviting speculation that perhaps it was the only cool thing in your wardrobe. In my case, the Stan Smiths *were* the only cool thing in my wardrobe. But they were shoes, and so wearing them every day, by eighth-grade norms circa 1984, was perfectly acceptable. The immigrant runs a sword through cost's belly every chance; the first-generationer instead puts the sword to its neck, letting it live, but ransoming outsized value for the mercy.

Let us set aside, however, these baser considerations. Let us know the object itself and see that it is good. The outside flank of a Stan Smith: simple, beautiful. The only pattern is holes. Very literally, then, design = function. There are smatterings of color, at top of heel and top of tongue: green. A bright, forthright green, the green of Bryce's lawn at an hour when the sun means business. Not a bullshit green—a hunter green, say, or a forest green or a racing green—which are all the same kinds of green, which is to say, green for people who are embarrassed of green and so don't deserve it. Those shades of green are as close as the color green can get to gray and still be green.

Even setting aside the particular shade, the

choice of green is striking. It marks a departure from the conventional blue of athleticism and the familiar red of competition. Nor is there a pair of colors to alleviate the seeming arbitrariness of this monotone. One thing connotes a thing; two or more things connote thingery. In musicals, the starlet spends much of the dance number between *two* escorting gentlemen so that the audience won't miss the choreography wondering distractedly, "*That* guy? Why that guy? Of all the guys, why that one particular guy?" Yet with Stan Smiths, it's just: here's some green. Years since his death and still we don't know whether Libyan dictator Muammar Qaddafi was clinically insane or advisedly savvy. Did he use a corps of female bodyguards called the Revolutionary Nuns out of non sequitur whimsy or because he believed Arab men wouldn't shoot a woman? Likely we'll never know. But the flag Qaddafi chose for his country — even understanding that green is a color associated with Islam, because multiple and unremarkable are the national flags of Muslim countries that incorporate green — was utterly singular. A solid rectangle of green. Nothing but green. This flag, like holed and one-hued shoes, said:

> Behold
> Here is this
> There is no else in this
> Only the what
> Itself
> Its self
> Behold
> The front of the shoe: still more impressive.

I'd seen a couple of kids with Stan Smiths. What caught my eye each time was the quarters—the eyelet-perforated wingflaps of leather through which the laces were strung. The quarters nearly met at the middle of the shoe. They left only a quarter-inch gap, revealing just the slightest strip of tongue underneath. In this way they resembled stage curtains and cathedral doors and rampart walls with a slot for a rifle barrel. They constituted that thing esteemed by the wealthy, and treasured by all humans, because all of us we die and sicken and weaken, we drift with entropy from our ideal selves, we need showers and shelter and all manner (clothing, laughing) of shameaway screens: conspicuous concealment. Even healthy and morning-fresh, we are swarmed over with flaws. Stendhal said beauty is the promise of happiness. That is true. It is also squalor's paint. The quarters hide the tongue that hides the foot that squirms monstrously underneath.

I don't know who Stan Smith was. I know he was a tennis player. I also know he once dusted a bucket of tennis balls with chalk and boasted to his doubles partner that he could hit every single ball onto a single spot on the other side of the court, with the chalk marks to prove it. His partner took him up on his boast, and Smith worked his way to the bottom of the bucket. After the last ball lofted and landed, Smith's partner gloated, pointing out that Smith had not merely failed to land every ball on the same spot—he'd managed to make a different mark with every ball. Smith, looking off at the tops of some trees, said, "Look closer." The doubles partner obliged. And that's

when he noticed the marks: chalk marks, perfectly spaced, in platen-rigorous lines, that spelled out a word:
SPOT.

When Smith's partner looked up again, Smith was yards away, already walking elsewhere, secure in his accomplishment without subsidy of praise.

None of this anecdote is true. I made it up. I could have done what everybody else does who claims casual knowledge of a subject. I could have skimmed the Wikipedia entry for Stan Smith and then typed out a paraphrasing and compared the original entry with my rendition and swapped out with synonyms all the still-remaining identical nonconnective verbs and modifiers. But take it as respect that, as between the vinyl facts of the Internet and the brain-bred leather of utter fabrication, I offer Stan Smith the latter. Arguably, it only honors the shoes. They're so good I feel like I owe something in the way of great admiration to this man I care nothing about. No offense to Mister Smith. But it's about the shoes.

A dance, right? A kind of dance, like the tango?
No.
They dance all the dances?
No.
Tap and ballet and belly —
No. Fancy dancing. Old-fashioned.
So it *is* a special kind of dance.
It's not a special anything. It sucks.
Shortly after I got my Stan Smiths, my father and I traveled to Greece. I'd been when I was two

but remembered nothing, so this was my dad's chance to show me the village where he was born and the country he had left. I wore my Stan Smiths in Greece. We mounted the Acropolis together, the Stans and me, and lapped the theater at Epidavros. When my uncle fished a sea urchin out of the same marina waters in Kounoupitsa where my father's father had docked the family boat, he knifed open the Star Trek–looking object and handed it to me. I slurped down the orange meat, and the Stans sampled a taste too because I had not paid enough attention to how my uncle, eating the first urchin, had while doing so thrust forward his body above the waist, like a conductor with a petulant orchestra, precisely so that shoes and pants would not be implicated.

In Greece, I insisted on wearing the Stans without socks, like all the rich kids did by the Bayshore. (Bayshore takes an article in Tampanian speech—"the Bayshore"—when used either metonymically to refer to the neighborhood radiating laterally from the boulevard or rhapsodically to the length of glamour and prestige that is the boulevard itself.) Socklessness may fly in Tampa—even in subtropical Tampa—but in Tampa we were students and so existed mostly behind a desk, and we were Floridians and so existed mostly in frigid air conditioning. Greece was different. I was a tourist. I existed almost entirely outside, tromping around with my father in hundred-degree heat. These exotic conditions forced my feet to superevolve in the span of a few days. They transmogrified from largely structural features into organs of perspiration. I perspired so much during that furnace of a trip that the sweat saturated the glues and linings and made the shoes reek foul. I pretended they didn't. My father wrenched me back to reality and said he'd met animal corpses that smelled better. When I started to debate the point, my father told me to grow up the best way a father can: not by telling me to grow up, but instead by reminding me that we were more than father and son, condemned by the onset of my adolescence to an ineluctable disalignment of interests; we were two men, roommates and fellow travelers, and obligated to be decent and mindful. Like Lord Byron in 1824, like Italian fascism in 1941, my Stan Smiths ended in Greece.

A couple of years ago, I tried on a pair of Stan Smiths. I've never lost a liking for their looks. But the shoes came freighted with memories: a new kid from New Jersey, a Spanish kid in South Tampa, a son of a hot dog vendor writing exclusively—by school mandate—in fountain-pen calligraphy. The shoes came redolent with urchin juice and foot reek. Also with a heady disbelief: in all the time I spent as an eighth-grader staring, amazed, at my genuine Stan Smiths made from unimpeachable cow, I could have invented an urchin bib, built a fried-okra replicator, and composed a musical about the Revolutionary Nuns. By adulthood, though, buying a pair felt more about simple admiration than hot and treacherous aspiration. I wasn't undertaking one of those fatuous youth-reclamation ventures that only prove counterproductively life-denying. I was just buying a nice pair of shoes.

I tried them on. They didn't look right. I untied

and retied them. Were these Stan Smiths? I
double-checked. Yes, they were. Problem: they
didn't look like Stan Smiths. Critically, the quarters didn't come anywhere near each other. They
barely covered the outer edges of the tongue,
which otherwise slobbered openly and heaved
up against the laces from ankle to vamp. Had
my feet changed? No. Not enough to explain
this. A widening of the foot extreme enough, rel-
ative to length, to yank apart the quarters by this
gruesome distance would have rendered the
shoe unwearable. No. Nope. These Stans were
nothing like a dauntless rampart. These Stans
were a guy asleep in his underwear, one leg
slung over the arm of a patio chair, an open bag
of Doritos smashed against his groin. I've tried a
few more pairs of Stan Smiths since then. Same
problem. Was there a magic at work here? Were
the Stans depriving me of concealment precisely
because, decades later, I didn't feel in need of it?
If so, why would I hate their looks so particular-
ly because they wouldn't do me the favor?

Why did Muammar Qaddafi refuse to climb
more than thirty-five steps at a time?

Payless ShoeSource, bankrupt, shuttered the
last of its stores last June. My sister, who still
lives in Tampa, visited the Armenia store the
day before it closed for good. While she browsed
an aisle, the manager, at the register, made an
abrupt decision and shouted to the floor floater
at the top of his lungs that they were going into
true liquidation mode.

¡Ahora vamos! ¡Siete pesos!

¡¿Por los zapatos?!

¡Y tres por las cualquieras!

¡¿Por las joyas, verdad?!

¡Si no son zapatos, los ponemos tres!

¡¿Y cuanto por los zapatos?!

¡Ay, por favor!

And the third felicity: my time with the Stans taught me, shaped me. I'm no rich kid from South Tampa. I can never forget the word *cotillion*, how pronounced with small vowels and a slight sustain on the *n* it telegraphs a breezy self-assuredness, yet when I wrote the word for this piece I could not help apprehending it as fundamentally alien, the type of thing with which my likes constitutionally lacked familiarity, and so felt compelled to look up the spelling. The word *swarthy* I still find complicated; it puts me in mind of the antisocial stench of sweat-fouled shoes. Sweaty, on the other hand, is ostensibly nonnormative. It is neutral, fact-bound. And the truth is, I am a sweaty Cuban-Greek kid from West Tampa. Socklessness? Not for me. Paylessness? Yes. More my style. Yes to paylessness.

I held my own in South Tampa. At our graduation dance, I danced with both Lauras. And that's like saying I shopped at the nicest mall in Tampa. Opposite worlds, it seems, merge all the time. In 2007, Payless ShoeSource Inc. acquired Sperry Top-Sider. The first time I heard this news, I didn't believe it. I still don't fully fathom it, given its sociocultural improbability. I'm doubting the Armenia Payless's evening shift had an easier time of it.

¡¿Mira, pero qué es esto?!

¡Sí, los zapatos nuevos, los *Toh-peh-sidee*!

¡¿Son como hechos de piel, o algo así?!

¡Claro, quizás, no sé! ¡Se llaman *eh-Sperri Toh-peh-sidee*!

¡¿De piel, como dos animalitos, verdad?!

¡Como dos cadáveritos, así mismo!

Do I miss Payless? I do. Do I mourn the fact I could not walk away one last time on its penultimate day of business? Not at all. I walked away from Payless in 1984, just as Stan Smith (didn't) stride off that chalk-scrawled court long ago, intent on the future, utterly un-nostalgic for what lay behind, not out of spite for the past but because he and I merely pine instead for what all lies ahead. We proceed with a certainty that has nothing to do with conviction—conviction for mortals made of sweat-sogged flesh is the same as arrogance and nonsense—and amounts more to a general hospitality, a decision to be decent to and mindful of the prospect that good things are around us and good things are to come.

We are venturers, Stan and I, sharing a particular certainty and a loose jaunty walk, a walk that says I'm from West Tampa, try it.

Why I Write

Few things are better than writing. Writing is sitting with coffee and hatching plans.

Many things are worse than not writing. But not writing is still pretty bad. It's a dark and reverse alchemy. It turns everything flat, plodding, resigned, airless. A light shove short of hopeless.

If we're going to count the reasons, then maybe it's three reasons I write. Because it's increasingly clear I'll never win an Olympic medal. And because Khubchand's balls. (Arundhati Roy's Khubchand was a very old dog. He still had two balls.)

I don't play competitive chess. Modern competitive chess, they say, is a memorization contest. Computers and rote learning mean the game nowadays is mostly scripted and executed according to recipe. Writing is the opposite. It has no parameters. It has no solution. It is thought made beautiful on a plate.

"10/31. Peter trick-or-treats as a policeman. We go to five houses total. But he's very proud of his haul. Afterwards at home, he takes inventory. With one exception — an Almond Joy — the candy is exactly the same candy we bought at Wal-Mart to give out to other kids. So we already have it. And he knows this. But he acts like it's the most exotic/enticing collection of candy he's ever seen. He is downright delighted. After dinner, he eats the Almond Joy, and Cathy and I watch.

GEORGE: How is it?

PETER: It's almonds, chocolate, coconut.

GEORGE: How do you like it?

PETER: Good.

GEORGE: How good?

PETER: As good as colored M&Ms.

GEORGE: Skittles?

PETER: Yeah.

CATHY: I thought Skittles were your favorite.

PETER: Almond Joy's as good as Skittles.

GEORGE: Is there anything you like more than Almond Joy and Skittles?

PETER: Daddy—

GEORGE: [I wait for him to finish, but he doesn't. So I repeat the question.] Is there anything you like more than Almond Joy and Skittles?

PETER: Daddy—

GEORGE: What?

CATHY: I think he's saying he likes Daddy more.

PETER: Daddy. [Walks over. Gives me a hug.]"

That Halloween my son was four years old. The above is what I wrote later the same night to remember the moment. Without writing I wouldn't have it.

Let other people in the world do worthwhile things, things of consequence, while I'm on Drugstore.com? I don't think so. The Germans surely have a word not for the campaign undertaken by a person convinced of its significance when a broader sense would make clear its triviality and emptiness, not for the campaigner's eventual realization that this is true, but for the mordant pathos, the vicarious humiliation, of another observing all this from a remove and realizing the truth before the campaigner does. I do not know this German word. I do not want to know it, for the slightest chance that thinking it will introduce its prospect like a virus into the bony round part at the top of my body.

Writing doesn't cost much. Running eats the knees and ballet pulps the feet. Sailing is how you farm melanomas. Stone sculpting: nerve damage. Blacksmithing: nerve damage. Lace tatting: not nerve damage; blindness. Writing costs the burning in my head maybe. It requires me to strip off the nice lies I wear the rest of life like a sweater. (When in history has anybody ever been simply fine?) Otherwise writing doesn't cost much at all. It's sweet and decent that way.

Writing lends immortality. Don't misunderstand. Writing doesn't grant immortality. Millions can speak your name after you're dead and it does nothing for the corpse. Writing just bestows immortality for a time. It lets you forget, for that blessed while, and rather completely, that one day you will die. It leavens what can feel like — what sometimes must be — the futility and desolation of life as it is lived. Hugh Nissenson's frontiersman understood the first part:

"Is Love as strong as Death?
I do not know.
Is Art?
My Art
Will raise the part of me
Writ here
Within some reader

In the year —
I do not care.
My life to come
Is now,
Within
This tune,
This flow."

David Mitchell's Robert Frobisher understood it all:

"How vulgar, this hankering after immortality, how vain, how false. Composers are merely
scribblers of cave paintings. One writes music
because winter is eternal and because, if one
didn't, the wolves and blizzards would be at
one's throat all the sooner."

I make up words. Beflouvinite, bicardia,
boomingest. People can't say no, can't mark
them red, can't imperialize their preferences,
can't indicate with a smug jut of the head their
looming friend with the twenty-one-inch biceps
named Merriam Webster. Dogstile, douche-
bag-shuhbag, dreamlet. Editor's house style?
Um, as my now echt-teenage son would put
it: Get that outta here. Words are the stuff of
thought. Language is the medium of existence
in any meaningful sense. And I make up that
shit entire. They have to publish them, they've
published all of them, because they come with
other, bigger chunks of more or less normal
words they actually do want to publish. Relent-
fully, reroosted, rodoucheo. Suckers.

Another reason to write: the possibility
of cobbling together a story wherein Robert
Frobisher runs into the frontiersman at, say, a
Sunglass Hut. They could teach each other a lot.

Assuming they didn't let their mutual bewilderment get the better of them. In that vein they
could teach us a lot.

I love writing because of the physicality of it.
Meaning there is no physicality of it.

I never decided the sound of my voice. My
large pores did not consult me. But people hold
me responsible. They say these are me. These are
no more me than the kid tugging on my jacket
in Aisle 9 of the Stop n' Shop because she's mistaken me for her dad. So much of me is appur-
tenance. So much of me is happenstance. What I
write, on the other hand, is very much me. Not
near me. Of me. My writing is more me than my
face.

—

I [Hard-Clenched Knuckle-Forward Fist] New York

—

THIS CITY IS FULL OF FIGHTS.

There is the man across the sidewalk from East 86th Street Cinemas.

He sells cheap wallets and phone cases and handbags. Early fifties, paunchy, shirt untucked. His beard is fitful. It's had more than enough time to come in, and it's done its best, and still it disappoints. His merchandise is laid across a folding table at the sidewalk's edge. There is more space between the items than any retailer would prefer. Parked in the street alongside the table is a peeling van with its side cargo door open. Inside the van are black garbage bags, lolling and flappy; inside the bags are white boxes. Sick grudging tongues and pills unswallowed.

There is the woman in her crisp forties standing across the sidewalk, her back to East 86th Street Cinemas. Not shabbily dressed. She has set her body square to the accessorymonger as if to make clear she will not let this go, she will not let him go, also sends looks like darts on the chance he has missed her meaning. But she breaks off eye contact after each look. (Which can mean fear. Which can also mean its haughty opposite. You can't tell yet. Keep watching.) Woman speaks into her phone, using a voice that tries for steadiness but allows itself to climb into indignation.

"Yeah, he's right here," she says.

"I'm looking at him right now," she says.

"I'm going to call the police."

"Eighty-Sixth Street, east of Third. On the south side."

"He's just standing there. Like it's nothing."

Man does not look at Woman. He does not turn in her direction. Instead he bustles around his table—across the front, around the sides, toward his van, back away from his van—and he puts a finger to the training beard and then withdraws it before it's had a chance at a meaningful stroke, whether because his exercised state prevents it or because he has resolved not to trespass upon that endangered flora, and since everybody knows that anybody who paces in public must also be heard to mutter, he mutters passionately, leaving as much space between the sentences as between his display pieces of nominal leather, of notional beard.

"I don't need that shit," he says. "Fuck that."

"Who you think I am?" he says. "Fuck, who you think you are?"

Everybody knows the longer the silence between mutters, the more deeply felt the sentiment.

"That bullshit. Fuck it, I don't need it. Fuck that."

Fuck it, you have to be somewhere, you keep walking.

This city starts fights. Unfair ones.

Unfair: lopsided, pitiably so, for reasons having nothing to do with their conduct.

Unfair: regrettable, entirely so, the two sides so wildly different that the notion they might fight — let alone that one might win — seems extravagant, spurious. What could they possibly have in common? What could they possibly have at stake?

There is the man outside the Papaya King on Third Avenue. His terms are simple:

"Dollar for coffee. Anybody got a dollar for a cup of coffee?"

But his pitch is far from it:

"It's my birthday today. Today is my birthday."

"Ain't anybody got a heart? None of these people got a heart."

"It's my birthday today. Nobody care it's my birthday."

He speaks in pairs of sentences, saying nearly the same thing in each member of the pair. It is scriptural verse. He is a prophet. He spends slightly more sentences talking about the state of people's hearts than about his price for laying off the condemnation.

There is the boy, on the corner, leaning against something with two of his friends. They wear white shirts, gray slacks, blue blazers. From a nearby private school. They look fourteen, which — given the exceptional nourishment that comes with privilege — means they're likely twelve. He calls out to the man.

"It was your birthday yesterday, too."

And: "How many birthdays have you had this week?"

You can tell from Boy's ramshackle grin, and from the fact he doesn't dare look straight at the man when he says these things, and from his careful positioning behind the head of his taller friend, that this child has no idea what he's talking about, that he has never before witnessed this man claim it was his birthday, that it very well may be this man's birthday, that while this man likely asks for money every day it is perfectly possible — indeed likely, given how vivid his claim, given how distinctive and therefore memorable and accordingly worthless for repeat use his claim — that he was in fact born on exactly this day thirty-odd years ago to a proud and glorying mother.

When his mouth moves, fumigating the passing crowd with guilt, Prophet ignores Boy altogether. When his mouth stills, Prophet fixes Boy with a glare — eyes at an angle, head and darkening sockets straight ahead. It is a glare for apostates, a registering of maximum disdain, a suggestion of greater ability than willingness to destroy. Boy keeps on. Prophet keeps on.

You keep on, you are going somewhere, you cannot know what happens next.

There is your friend Jodi, who has it figured out. Her premises are as follows:

You cannot give to all who ask. You should not give to none at all. The disabled are deserving but unverifiable. A man, all else equal, can offer manual labor. A woman, all else equal, will be pushed to offer something else.

Her solution is a rule: give to every woman who asks.

It is simple, reasoned, noble. You adopt the rule yourself. You resolve to give accordingly.

Except the very next day, when you pass a

woman begging whom you recognize from before you adopted the rule as a woman who for months has begged regularly, sometimes daily, on the sidewalks that lead to and from your office. If you give her something today, you'll have to give her something every day. You are a wage worker, not a micro-bank.

Except a week after, because the woman begging near Grand Central is twenty rivers of commuters away from you and — maybe this is an engineering problem, maybe this is not a defect of the heart — with which do you retrieve a wallet when left hand lugs a gym bag and right hand a laptop?

Except a third time, and you don't remember the exact woman or the exact location, nor do you remember your reasons for not taking out your wallet, but the latter failure of recollection is enough to persuade you the reasons were shoddy.

One month after adoption and you have succeeded once. You gave one woman a ten dollar bill. The 1-3 win-loss record is dispiriting. So is the possibility you gave her a ten not out of generosity but to ease the dispiritment.

This city is a fight.

Right? This is what New York is, finally, isn't it? An unfair fight? Every soul in the city against the city itself. Gray above, gray below, and between these the press of humanity struggling for humanity. A teeming crowd, at once intent and oblivious, at once living and inert. We love our anonymity and yet we hate our separateness. We crave our dignity and mourn that it takes someone known to us to recognize it.

The thing with Man and Woman, the thing with Prophet and Boy: you do not like to re-member these happened just one half-block away from each other, just hours apart on the same day. Just five days before Christmas.

The woman who sold you an indulgence at the right reasonable price of ten dollars: you've never seen her again.

City always wins.

The Vengeances

Paris steals Helen. Pries her out of her husband's bed, seasons her lips with his own, spirits her to Troy.

Of course that's how it starts. Love is the seed of every perfidy, of every cataclysm. Even the chaste kind has its spawn.

Paris's, hardly chaste, sires the world's longest feud:

(1) 1184 B.C. — GREEKS: The Greeks take first vengeance. They burn Troy to the ground. There is talk in Homer of babies thrown from the tops of walls. The Greeks probably shouldn't have done that.

(2) 753 B.C. — ITALIANS: Round two. Aeneas, the vaunted Trojan, escapes destruction. He flees to the Italian peninsula. His descendants found Rome. If the best revenge is living well, there is no defter comeuppance than founding an empire.

(3) 325 B.C. — GREEKS: Except founding an empire that nuzzles India. Alexander the Great makes traditional notions of conquest, and Romans, look ridiculous. Point, Greeks.

(4) 27 B.C. to 476 A.D. — ITALIANS: And in that, I confess, I take a little delight. Because — full disclosure — I am Greek. Half-Greek, actually. My Greek father ran a sandwich shop in an office park. I helped (notionally) with phone orders and food prep, sometimes cash register.

I did not wear anything close to the smile my father insisted be presented to customers. Once, a manager from the medical supply outfit on the other side of the building ordered a meatball sub. While waiting he spied on the back counter a titanic can of the Neptune-brand tuna my father used. He knew my father was Greek. I'm guessing he saw an opportunity (this in the either callow or halcyon—pick one based on your age—days before search engines) to scratch a longstanding itch.

"If Poseidon is god of the sea, who is Neptune?" the customer asked.

"Neptune," my father replied quietly, undemonstratively, with the substrate conviction of one trafficking in axioms, "is Poseidon's helper."

Well, for centuries after Alexander's corpse turns to livid soil, Rome burgeons and conquers and prospers. Neptune is decidedly *not* anyone's helper. Neptune leaves Poseidon polled and clipped and moaning in a watery corner. Never are tears more futile than when shed directly into ocean.

Point, Italians.

(5) 326–1000 A.D. — GREEKS: The Byzantine Empire displaces the Roman. It also reigns as the world's mightiest religious institution. Empress Helena herself discovers the True Cross—the wood on which Jesus was crucified—after being led by the scent of basil to the patch of ground where it lies buried.

To honor the miracle, basil is thereafter revered by the Greeks. Many refuse to ingest it as food because of its spiritual significance. I once pressed my father on why he did not eat basil. He is an avid churchgoer in the sense that the post-liturgy coffee hour is indeed held in a church building.

"For the same reason you don't eat horse," he said.

"I don't eat horse because Kash n' Karry doesn't sell horse," I said.

He gave me the same look as when I wasn't smiling enough at customers.

(6) 1054 A.D. — ITALIANS: The Pope sends an obstreperous cleric to Constantinople. Cardinal Humbert's mission: to finally reconcile the Latin and Greek churches. The Cardinal instead antagonizes the Greek Patriarch. The two bicker about whether communion bread should be leavened.

Humbert has a fit and leaves. But not without a flourish. First he lays down a papal bull on the altar of the Greek cathedral. The Greeks are excommunicated.

Later, the Pope repudiates Humbert's tantrum. He claims the Bull was never authorized. He does not, however, withdraw it. Nor does he explain the entrusting of diplomacy to a cantankerous sorehead. It is like sending a tarantella band to soothe a baby.

(7) 1182 A.D. — GREEKS: The new Byzantine emperor sanctions a massacre of the Latins in Constantinople. He is deposed and murdered three years later. Some are sure his fate is repayment for wholesale murder in a holy city. They have no idea.

(8) 1204 A.D. — ITALIANS: The Venetians commandeer the Fourth Crusade. They forgo Muslim targets and sack Constantinople instead.

This is repayment. Thousands are slaughtered.
Masses of holy relics are looted. A fragment of
the True Cross, stolen from the emperor's private chapel, returns west with the victors.

All this transpires after Pope Innocent III's
blessing of the crusade. He had hoped to install
a Rome-friendly emperor. But the bloodbath
must be disavowed. The Pope recycles an excuse
from 1054: none of it was authorized. Thus he
transubstantiates himself into a rebus — the "III"
representing the fringing lashes of a winking eye
just after the word *innocent* is pronounced.

Occhio per occhio.

(9) 1261 A.D. — GREEKS: The Greeks re-
take Constantinople. The Latins are expelled.
The original relics, of course, cannot be restored.
But facsimiles begin to resurface in all the same
places. These "reappearances" are explained as
miracles. It is a net positive: relics no longer lost,
a rich new body of devotional narrative in the
bargain.

What the Greek does not have, he wills.

Odónta antí odóntos.

(10) 1453 A.D. — ITALIANS: Of all the
world's feuds, few rival that between Greek and
Latin. One contender: the long-running debacle
between Greek and Turk. Its wounds, especially
among older generations, are startlingly fresh.
At dinner in 1985, when I was a high school
freshman, I chattily informed my father that I'd
signed up for Model United Nations. The meal
ended with my father informing me — shaking
his head in a way that carried some of the shoulders with it — that I was mistaken, that in fact I
had signed up for nothing. He issued this pro-

nouncement after asking me, not once but twice, to repeat the part about how the school's team would be representing Turkey.

The next day I told the MUN moderator a piano recital had come up last-minute, the way piano recitals sometimes (never) do.

For centuries Byzantium staves off Islamic conquest. For centuries the Greeks shelter behind Constantinople's famous walls. Even on Tuesday, May 29, 1453, when sixty thousand Ottomans and mercenaries mass outside the city, the walls hold. The Turks do not breach them. But, it turns out, they do not need to. A Genoese general fighting for the Greeks has demanded that a single gate be unlocked so that he might abscond to his ship.

The Turks find the gate. They pour in after Giovanni Giustiniani and his retreating contingent.

One Italian's desperation becomes every Greek's catastrophe. The Turks take the capital and the empire. For hundreds of years after 1453, the Greeks live in slavery, subjects of the Ottoman sultanate.

A few years ago I reminded my father about his forbidding me from representing Turkey at a school event. He is in his eighties now. I asked him if, looking back, he thought that was the right thing to do. He shrugged his shoulders, the same shoulders that in 1985 had loomed like bulwarks against the possibility of appeal, and said simply, "I don't know. But it was too much to ask."

Five and a half centuries after that fateful Tuesday, one and a half centuries after liberation, and still my father speaks in terms of insufferable burden.

(11) 1500s to 1600s A.D. — GREEKS: Rome dominates the Christian faith, dispatches it to three new continents. Still, the Greeks persist in their differences. They continue to reject, for instance, the Catholic communion wafer. They cite historical fidelity and maintain that only leavened bread can stand in for Christ's body. This candidactism is in fact an act of mercy. The hungrier the communicant, and so the more freely salivating, the less likely that prim and stinting disk survives long enough to be chewed.

As a teenager I took comfort in this notion one Wednesday a month. That was when my Jesuit high school held mandatory mass. We had time during these services for quiet contemplation, the Jewish kids and I, when at Communion we perched in our pews and watched our schoolmates file out to the priests and their wafers and file back. I had every opportunity to mull the incongruences between Greek and Catholic worship. There existed a serious discrepancy, for example, regarding the provenance of the Holy Spirit. I'd always understood that it proceeded from the Father. That's what the Creed I'd recited from boyhood said. Yet every Wednesday in St. Anthony's Chapel roughly 615 people disagreed, reciting a different version of the Creed — 15 in registers resonant with Jesuit aplomb and mastery, 600 in pubescent murmurs suggestive of hour-long indenture — in which the Holy Spirit proceeded also from the Son.

At some point I learned something that cheered me. The Greeks had long ago spurned the *Filioque* as theologically unsound, as surplusage bolted on unilaterally by the Catholics nearly eight hundred years after Christ. I came to enjoy this moment in the Creed. Every Wednesday I reveled in silence while the rabble droned their trisyllabic blasphemy: *and the Son.* It came at the end of a sentence and so sounded like superfluous prattle. The anapest rhythm, moreover, implied a blunder — words absently blurted and later regretted.

(12) 1687 A.D. — ITALIANS: The Venetians attempt to dislodge the Turks from Greece. The Greeks, two centuries into Ottoman subjugation, let their hopes soar. But ultimately the Venetians fail. In the attempt, however, they do succeed in bombarding the Acropolis to bits.

When the world looks at the Parthenon, it sees the temple that still stands: a monument to humanity's greatest achievements.

When the Greeks look at the Parthenon, they see also the parts that have fallen away. The view is no less wondrous. Like every dashed hope, it is a sad and beautiful ruin.

(13) 1757 and 1810 A.D. — GREEKS: The Church of the Holy Sepulchre in Jerusalem is the holiest church in Christendom. Inside it are the sites of Jesus's crucifixion and burial. Empress Helena oversaw its construction. It was during excavations for this building that she smelled basil and found the True Cross.

For centuries, six sets of Christians have struggled over control of the Church: Catholics, Greeks, Armenians, Copts, Ethiopians, and Syrians. They live side by side inside the building — but in an anxious pique. Each obsessively preserves historical claims over particular rooms and walls and inches of floor. Each watches carefully for where the others make repairs or leave their brooms, because even these might be the basis for future claims. A ladder propped alongside the top-right window over the main entrance has leaned there since 1854. No agreement has ever been reached on how, or even whether, it might be moved.

From time to time, fights erupt among the priests and monks. Robes flap, beards fly. It is a wonder the queues of pilgrim visitors have not included quantities of Taiwanese parliamentarians. They would feel at home here.

In 1757, the Ottomans, fearing a Russian invasion, award primacy at the Church to the Greeks. The Greeks get Christ's tomb; the Catholics get a scattering of lesser chapels. Czar Nicolas and his fellow Orthodox are placated. The Pope and his followers, on the other hand: not pleased.

In 1808, the building is devastated by fire. By 1810, it is restored. But now the Greek spaces are larger — in exactly the same places where the common areas are smaller. Also, many of the Latin markers and decorations are now Greek. It happens that the architect for the renovation was a man by the name of Nikolaos Komnenos. From Mytilene. A Greek.

The Greeks probably shouldn't have done that.

(14) 1863 A.D. — ITALIANS: If the best revenge is served cold (the sheer number of bromides about revenge is weird, but those nurturing resentments and awaiting opportunities

own the perfect confluence—fever and free time—for authoring a thing or two), then the Italians finally manage to surpass their own high mark of empire founding. It takes them more than a half-century to retaliate. Not until 1863 is the cookbook *La Cuciniera Genevese* published. Inside is the first written evidence of that cunning and magnificent travesty: pesto. Here is the recipe.

Take Greece's holy plant. Do not merely shred or dice it. *Pound* it into a paste. Adulterate this new substance with pig food: pine nuts. Add a malodorous cheese—Parmesan, Pecorino, Romano, it doesn't matter, because what's important is to so corrupt Saint Helena's beloved scent that it turns against itself, from poignant to pungent. Finally, slick this mealy abomination with copious amounts of oil, so that you and your guests turn it as quickly as possible into shit.

Basil, when heated, blackens and goes bitter.

The fourteenth vengeance, therefore, is best served cold.

(15) 4:00 a.m., October 28, 1940 A.D. — GREEKS: The Italian ambassador thinks it a good idea to present the leader of Greece with an ultimatum. Surely Mussolini himself, chafing to found a new Roman empire, has commanded it. Surely Mussolini used his famous signature posture when giving the order—chin thrust forward and up.

The threat comes on October 28, 1940. Submit to Axis occupation, warns the Italian ambassador, or face war. Ioannis Metaxas reportedly answers with a single word: *Ohi*. No.

The Greeks still celebrate Ohi Day every October. Mainly they honor the laconic defiance in that single word. No stauncher proof of a readiness to fight than keeping talk to a minimum.

But anyone who has been to Greece, or Astoria, Queens, or Tarpon Springs, Florida, might guess the real reason for the day's immortality. If you've seen a Greek say no, you've seen him do it in the iconic Greek fashion. Whether or not the word itself is spoken, whether or not (as is often the case) the tongue is instead unglommed abruptly from the palate with percussive disdain — with that sound of a blood-wet switch regrettably transliterated in the English-speaking world as "tsk" but more obviously resembling "tch" — always that negating Greek chin is thrust forward and up.

Ohi Day is not a mere remembrance. It is a living caricature of Italy's most notorious leader. It is a cue for derision on a national scale. "It does not matter that once you hung him upside down," a whole country is saying; "we and our chins will mock him, right side up, in perpetuity."

It is an evergreen humiliation.

(16) 5:30 a.m., October 28, 1940 A.D. — ITALIANS: Mussolini attacks later the same morning. The assault lasts months.

(17) 1940–1941 A.D. — GREEKS: There is one radio in my father's village of Kounoupitsa. It belongs to Ioannis Dedegikas. When Ioannis is in a good mood, he sets it on his balcony and turns up the volume. Neighbors gather underneath to hear news of the fight against the

Italians. Some are drawn to the understated glamour of the BBC. Others prefer the strident tones of the Free Voice of Greece, the mouthpiece of Greece's government-in-exile in Egypt; its broadcasters manage to speak in a kind of perpetual call, sounding exactly as far away as across the sea.

The rest of Kounoupitsa gets their war news from the church bell. A slow tolling means a Greek defeat. A fast pealing means a victory. Who knows who rings the bell — the priest himself? His wife? Not his son. His son has gone to war.

The villagers hear more peals than tolls. So many peals, in fact, that it's hard to believe. One imagines the villagers starting to suspect the accuracy of the ringing. One imagines them joking that the priest's wife is purposely botching the job so her son will have to return from the front to take over.

But no. The peals are accurate. The Greeks are prevailing. They do not simply resist. They repel. They counterattack and chase the Italians into Albania. It is a rout.

Hitler asks the Italians to withdraw from Greece altogether. Like children bold with sugar and capering in a driveway, they are urged to get out of harm's way. The Panzers will take it from here.

(18) 1941 A.D. — ITALIANS: Two men from Kounoupitsa die at the lines. One is a seventeen-year-old named Nikos Javelas. The other is the priest's son.

The bodies are never brought back from the front.

The priest and his wife carry on. Nikos's mother does not. For the rest of her life, she wanders the village, moaning the same words over and over. *Niko mou, se afisane sto krio*. My Niko, they left you in the cold.

The Germans occupy key locations: Athens, Thessaloniki, Crete. The Italians get the leftovers. In the Italian zone there is looting. Worse, too. Depredations mount with desperation. Generally, their egregiousness runs inversely to their distance from the cities. Kounoupitsa sits in the hilltops of Methana, a peninsular bit of volcanic land that points like Diogenes's lantern from the Peloponnesus toward Athens. My father remembers mostly chicken theft.

(19) 1947 A.D. — GREEKS: The war dust settles. Greece reclaims the islands of the Dodecanese. This ends a thirty-five-year Italian occupation. There is only one downside. Arguably this vindicates the Italians. They had always insisted on describing their takeover as "temporary."

(20) 1954 A.D. — ITALIANS: Before he owns a sandwich shop, before he comes to the United States, my father is a ship captain. He starts his merchant marine career as a *naftis*—a deckhand. His first ship is the *Maria*. It has only one route: Piraeus, Greece to Trieste, Italy, and back again. The *Maria* is a cargo shuttle. From Greece to Italy, it carries *alefopetra*, a lightweight stone used then in construction materials. From Italy to Greece, it carries hay.

My father remembers lots of things about the *Maria*—how the captain and the owner both discovered he knew English (at the time a mark of some distinction), how the captain thereafter replaced all his duties with just one (paperwork), how the owner thereafter invited him to lunch after lunch to discuss his marriageable niece (my father, wily as Odysseus, implying just enough interest to keep the lunches coming).

But most of all my father remembers gelato.

Every night in Trieste, he and the rest of the crew eat gelato. Every night the Greeks place their orders, and the Italians behind the counter ask "*E*?" and the Greeks—oblivious that the custom is to request two flavors, served side by side—merely smile as if remembering picnics with their favorite aunts. The Italians give up. Apparently convinced all Greeks love lemons, they foist on these gruff and daft customers, every one of them, a second flavor of lemon.

The crew stroll about as they enjoy their gelato. They admire the clean streets. They envy the city's easy vigor, its magic of liveliness without crowds or traffic. They watch the passing women, fully appreciating the impossibility of looking manly while delighting in gelato. They manage anyway.

Having brought with them stones lighter than stone and eaten ice cream lighter than ice cream, the Greeks head home aboard the *Maria*. Amid the affable huff of aging diesel engines they feel lighter, more hopeful, than when they arrived.

This was Italy's vengeance: it bewitched my father. His first taste of the ships had the flavor of promise, of perfection. That happenstance of gorgeous Trieste, of wonderful gelato, of counterwomen who smiled back like *they* were the favorite aunts: by golden association, they

ensnared my father into a long merchant marine
career, nearly derailed his larger dream of coming to America.

It is a small vengeance, though. Really my
father's stories of Trieste are less about rivalry
than about sweet commiseration. Whenever
my father tells them, I see two countries, one as
war-broken and impoverished as the other, trad-
ing rocks and grass between them. Each offers
the other what it can: parts of itself.

(21) August 2, 1968 A.D. — GREEKS: The
Katingo lies in port at Genoa, Italy. It is a 16,000-
ton oil tanker. My father is captain.

Onto the ship struts a man my father has
never met. My father knows only two things
about this stranger: he arrives fresh from a honeymoon on a lake in Austria, and he is taking
over command of the *Katingo.*

My father is resigning his captaincy. In just
over a month, he will take a train from Piraeus,
board a Luxair jet to New York, and emerge
from JFK International Airport's Arrivals Hall
into a new life. The stranger coming aboard is
the *Katingo*'s new captain.

For a man with larger concerns, my father
spends an inordinate amount of time consider-
ing his successor. Specifically, he believes he will
be a disaster. A captain who honeymoons on a
lake in Austria does not know how to speak to
a *lostromos,* a bosun, whose family's only asset
is a mule. A captain who honeymoons on a lake
in Austria does not know how to say enough
is enough when a seller's representative insists
that Tank #4 be washed a fifth time, or how to
manipulate this representative with a particu-

lar cocktail of geniality and menace into feeling shrill and fatuous and unreasonable, or how to finally appear to give in and just provide the requested signature—but with the sneaky and nullifying words "subject to owner's approval" underneath—when the representative demands, abashedly, defensively, that the ship at least assume the risk of contamination from Tank #4's uncleanable muck.

It is important that Italy was both my father's first destination as a seaman and his last. It made the contrast all the sharper. In his first port, the air itself smelled of sweet destiny. In his last, the grinning and obsequious ship chandler brought aboard a local introduced only as "Dominick" who proposed that my father sail loads of cigarettes after sunset to boats waiting just inside international waters. In Trieste, there were smiling passersby. In Genoa, there were grim-faced insurance inspectors who insisted on seeing the lifeboats lowered and raised and lowered again, because this is the subtle semaphore with which dandies suborn their bribes—*We can do this the easy way or the hard way*. In Trieste, the world waited at happy heel. In Genoa, the groveling chandler listened intently as my father, in one of his last acts as captain, ordered two cases of Coca-Cola (along with coffee, the standard hospitality beverage aboard Greek ships at the time) and then promptly ignored the request because a soon-to-be-former captain is the same as nothing.

Life for everyone, to some degree, is a trip from Trieste to Genoa. Life hardens under the press of responsibility and striving, shrinks to fit the strictures of routine and expectations betrayed, wears from the constant scanning for threats and mustering of wherewithal. The blush of promise turns—even as we mourn its loss, even as we protest it needn't be this way— into the uncleanable muck of necessity and mediocrity and compromise.

We all collect our wounds and retreat to Genoa.

Forty years later, my father will drive his Ford Econoline E-150 cargo van on a bimonthly basis from his Tampa home to a shop on Florida Avenue. The shop sits directly across the street from ABC Auto Sales and alongside Fried Rice King. There he gets his hair cut for twelve dollars by a Vietnamese woman named Kim. Often she will ask him—half in jest, half in deference to profit—if he's sure he won't try a manicure. Each time my father, without willing it, thinks of the captain fresh from his honeymoon on a lake in Austria. One pristine hand grips a deck rail. The other tightens with clear-coat nails the line around a seaman's waist before sending him across a storm-tossed deck to secure a pair of loose steel pipes.

The honeymooner keeps silent. A good captain cannot. A good captain says, nodding at the rope line, *This will keep you safe.* Because he has to. Because everyone knows it's really so that a mother will have something to bury, so that she'll not haunt a village with wails and wandering.

(22) September 2002 A.D. — ITALIANS: I marry an Irish American from Ossining, New York. She is Roman Catholic. The wedding is

in her childhood parish. My mother makes me swear that after the honeymoon we'll have a Greek Orthodox ceremony at my own childhood parish in Tampa. It will be a brief ceremony, a kind of blessing. My mother makes this request not because she cares, but because my father otherwise would pretend not to.

I accede for the same reason a Trieste counterwoman could simply dispense a double serving of a single flavor but would never dream of it. Tradition is important.

For the honeymoon my wife chooses Italy. In Venice we stay at the Danieli because we cannot afford to, and that goes far in making it a honeymoon.

A few hours after check-in, Cathy drops her wedding ring into the bathroom sink. She peers down the drain and sees nothing. I peer down the drain and see the gently graying, utterly soigné salesman at David S. Diamonds standing behind the vitrines with a replacement ring in one hand and my 18.99% APR MasterCard in the other, pinching the latter between thumb and index because, shriveled, it now resembles the torn corner of a page from a very sorry ledger.

The front desk sends a maintenance man, who dismantles the undersink assembly. In moments he finds the ring and bluffly hands it over. He receives a tip worth one one-thousandth the ring's value.

Twelve years later I will learn that during a festival every spring, in a millennium-old tradition, the mayor of Venice (and before him the *doge*) drops a wedding ring into the sea. This is how Venice celebrates its marriage to the ocean.

At checkout I review the bill. The bottom line is an injury, the comma between numbers a dagger. The top is insult: staring out at me from the letterhead are the four famous bronze horses of St. Mark's basilica, looted by the Venetians from Constantinople in 1204.

(23) November 2002 A.D. — GREEKS: The parking lot at St. John's Greek Orthodox is not huge. When we arrive one Saturday morning, therefore, it is easy to see the priest is not there. In fact, he arrives fifteen minutes late. (Promptness for a Greek is disrespect for tradition. We are five minutes late ourselves.) While family and friends fill the pews with chatter and fundament, the priest pulls my wife and me into an office, briefs us hastily on the ceremony—mostly bullet points on choreography—and answers "Yes, yes" to a question from my wife that begins "Where." This persuades us against the utility of further questions.

When the ceremony begins, we know to face the priest. We know that much. What we don't know—because no one has told us, because though once I was an altar boy I never had cause to learn there are only weddings in the Greek church and no such thing as "wedding blessings"—is that we're in for a full-blown wedding, complete with wedding crowns and three processions around the altar.

What we also don't know: *to take off our wedding rings*. After speaking a few lines to launch the ceremony, the priest regards the two of us warmly, leans in, and asks, "Do you have the rings?" My wife and I have the same reaction;

we cram our ringed hands against our stomachs while using our other hands to torque the rings off, careful to smother our elbows against the sides of our bodies because, unaccountably but passionately, we both believe that disallowing air between arms and abdomen will somehow ensure invisibility. It is a caricature of surreptitious movement. It is a caricature performed in tandem, moreover, and on the equivalent of a stage, making it that much more ridiculous. When the priest sees those rings, he freezes, his mouth hardens — the warmth is gone — and he looks up at us and stares, and we realize our error not least because the other thing that happens is that the burl of his nose, already pocked and creased and notched, now crinkles in addition, as if catching the stench of apostasy rising off our fourth fingers.

These details do not concern my father. He sits in a pew quite satisfied. He once sailed a Pacific route where a nighttime transit through the Panama Canal found the crew so exhausted that they humiliated themselves by taking turns trying and failing to heave a half-inch line to a waiting tugboat; where he stranded himself and six ailing crew members in Tokyo after navigating them to a prearranged clinic visit but then missing the rendezvous time with the ship; where the ship encountered a typhoon so violent, and swamping seas so massive, that continuing ahead seemed like sure disaster, and turning seemed like certain catastrophe, and the ship — equally sensitive to this predicament — took forty-five seconds, engines full ahead and rudder hard starboard, to decide finally to turn.

For my father, the challenges of the journey are inevitable and irrelevant. He has reached the appointed harbor.

The second wedding reception is at Maggiano's Little Italy. The Greek priest is invited but does not come. I do not know that these facts are related.

In sum: I am Greek. But I have never lived in Greece. I do not speak Greek. My identity and provenance are a patchwork of remnants: family vacations in Athens and Methana spent drinking frappes made with instant Nescafé; weekly duty as altar boy, during which hunks of bread were so roundly pilfered by the acolyte crew that the prophylactic antitheft properties of the Catholics' savorless chip are ingenious in retrospect; Sunday School with Fifi Russell, a sweet-tempered woman with enormous spectacles that magnified her eyes into wonder-struck saucers and encased them in a fog that suggested the brink of emotion, who taught that anyone we encountered could be Jesus in disguise, testing our good will; Greek dance practice, wherein the boys constantly maneuvered to link hands with the only blonde girl, courtesy of the Ukrainian Orthodox mother for whom a Greek church was the only game in town; my father's stories. Cultural totems — an esteem for basil, an unrepentant tardiness — are the prosthetics of the first generation. We seize on them heartily, take them everywhere we go, because they animate the vestiges we've inherited. For me, these totems are a large part of my Greekness. For my father they are fusty and faintly ridiculous and smell like the inside of a favorite aunt's purse. He lived Greece. His memory is soused with it. He has no need for tropes. In the end, his avoidance of basil is a habit, really, and not much more.

My son is named after my father, in the Greek tradition. But my son's name is "Peter," what my father called himself after arriving in this country. It is not "Panagiotis," my father's birth name. Even names are an approximation.

One wonders what happens to the Greek identity after a generation or two. One wonders whether the identity proceeds from the father and the son, or just the father. I am, after all, a man who honeymooned on a lagoon in Venice.

My bride is Roman Catholic. The Italian sea stole her during our honeymoon and married her in the U-bend of a porcelain-enameled drain trap. Both my children are baptized Roman Catholic. We live in Westchester County, in fact a collection of Italian neighborhood restaurants with just enough homes and businesses to supply a clientele, and just enough trees and grass to dilute the scent of adulterated basil.

Of course that's how it ends.

Love is the fruit of every perfidy, of every cataclysm.

Match, Italians?

Ohi. A Greek never capitulates. Not ever.

—

87th & Abomination

—

THE BEST BAKERY I'VE EVER KNOWN WAS AN OLD German one. Glaser's, on First and 87th. It sat in the heart of Yorkville, the Manhattan neighborhood settled early in the twentieth century by émigrés from the former Prussian empire. It was reputed, among other things, to have invented the black-and-white cookie.

Glaser's was my favorite for three reasons.

First, the things there tasted good in my mouth. The black-and-white was spectacular. The black-and-white wasn't even the sixth best thing they made.

Second, it was unpretentious. Perhaps this matter-of-factness, this forthrightness, was a Lutheran cultural inevitability. The lights pointed down, not up. They sold things for cost plus a reasonable margin rather than turning everything into a Louis Vuitton version of itself. The website had as many interactive features as the tile floor inside. (To be clear, the tile floor, like other tile floors, had no interactive features.)

Third, it was heaven. And this I mean literally.

Visits to bakeries come with a catch. You want what smells so great. But, of course, you can't have what smells so great, because what smells so great, uncoincidentally, is everything in combination. Bakery Scent is a complex that cannot be dismantled or piecemealed. No single pastry, no isolated treat, can deliver what the omnibus fragrance promises. Result: however delightful the cake or cruller consumed, one must always leave a bakery quietly dismayed that one can't have what one truly wants. This poignant tease, this ineluctable shortfall, is on purpose: so that we mortals, flawed and grasping, should never experience heaven on earth. As the conceivable Lutheran teaching presumably goes (I say "conceivable" and "presumably" because I do not know of such a teaching; I was born Greek Orthodox, and enjoy cake more than ecumenical history, and so am wildly speculating here): we may know the sacred; we may not possess it.

Glaser's was different in this respect. Exceptional. The women behind the counter knew exactly how good everything was, and they wanted everybody to know it, and so, as you took steps to procure for yourself and the family a bag of black-and-white cookies, they made sure you also tasted sample after sample of the nutfree brownie and the nutful brownie, the almond cookie and the chocolate coconut cookie, the raspberry crumb bar and the blueberry graham loaf and the gingerbread sheet cake. They wanted you to taste and see that the Lord was good. In short, you experienced at Glaser's what Lutherans surely possibly believe the natural law forbids: you tasted exactly everything that smelled so great.

One Friday afternoon I found myself in the line that stretched from sidewalk to back counter and then curled around to the side counter where orders were taken. In front of me waited

a man in his twenties. When between him and
the counter-angels stood only two customers, he
turned to me. This is what he said:

"What's good here?"

I stared at him. I opened my mouth. I did not
know the good words to tell to him, or how to be
making the words. Finally two came out, quiv-
ering: "You don't."

Likely he thought I was asking him prelimi-
narily to confirm he didn't know what to order.
In fact I was staggered: by his innocence, by the
daunt of explaining in a few puny seconds the
momentousness of his opportunity, by the fact
he had no idea where he was. Too much for
one humble cake-lover to bear. I gazed at him
as from behind an impregnable plasma of neu-
ron fire. This dazzled remove was the stun of
my own brain, showering the same transfixing
thought in series and series of series. You don't
even know. You don't even know.

We may know the sacred; we may not im-
part it.

I told him to close his eyes and point and
order that. I said this glib thing as gently as I
could. Deeply I wanted him to understand it
not as haughty castigation but as the truth, plain
and earnestly meant. He laughed, then gave me
that assessing look that lasts a bit longer without
speech than is consistent with social nicety before he turned back around. Either I had gotten
through to him or I had convinced him I was the
nutful kind versus the nutfree.

He ordered the black-and-whites.

Glaser's closed a few years ago, for good.
The baker got tired of waking up at three. There

was no next generation to take over.

It is the kind of loss that spills and spills. I smell cake from an amateur oven and I remember. I go to other bakeries and they make me sad because I remember.

Glaser's made a cinnamon danish from a hundred-year-old recipe. It will take me an equal number of years to recover. May God, whether deuterocanonical or otherwise, help me.

The Petervian Calendar

The Year I Sleep So Little I Remember It Only as a Gray Curtain	Peter is born.
The Year He Follows Me Around Everywhere	Peter and I walk to the playground down the street and hop onto the swings. We bore quickly of rote pendulum motion. We invent Battleswing, a martial-themed game that awards a point each time a player—er, war-rior—succeeds in touching his foot against the opponent swinging alongside him, so long as foot contact is made with the other's legs above the knees (lower legs are too accessible and gut the game of challenge) or with the front or back of his trunk. Safety is paramount: contact with head, neck, or arms is prohibited; holding on with both hands is mandatory. I learn three things. First, at the playground that day, I learn that three-year-olds lack the neural pathways to distinguish between foot contact and kicking. Second, in bed the next morning, I discover a sullen bruise at the center of my lower back, the very place where birthing mothers sometimes experience bruising from epidur-als. Mothers pay with their bodies through parturition, it seems, and fathers after. Third, at the same playground six months later, it dawns on me—as multiple mothers shoot aren't-we-setting-a-bad-example looks in my direction—that if safety were really paramount, there would be no such thing as Battleswing.

| The Year I Have Bad Ideas, Very Like Unto the Years Before and Also After | It snows eight inches.
I shovel, Peter plays.
Once I finish, we drift onto the front lawn. It is a mattress of snow.
I point at two trees, ask Peter if he remembers using them once as a soccer goal (he does), and propose I curl up like a ball and he try to kick me through the snowfield into the goal.
He likes this idea; it involves kicking and/or foot contact.
I like this idea; it involves the madcap spontaneity that commercials for credit cards and cruise lines suggest middle-aged suburbanite fathers should be exhibiting more often.
Peter scores two goals.
It is great fun. Until he kicks me in the penis.
It gets dark suddenly, for reasons having nothing to do with the sun. |

| The Year After the Year I Realize What Everybody Else Already Knows, Which Is That It Is, Always Has Been, Me Following Him Around Everywhere | Friday before Columbus Day Weekend. Peter has the day off from school, so I take a vacation day myself. We put on shorts and bring his bicycle and my waveboard to the playground and play Cops & Robbers. As I chase him, tottering atop what is essentially a two-wheeled skateboard, Peter turns his bicycle into me rather than away from me, and at speed. I have two choices and one moment to make them: (1) bail from the waveboard and get out of the way to minimize the impact but thereby run the risk that he catches his front tire on my abandoned waveboard and catapults over the handlebars, or (2) stand my ground and absorb the impact by grabbing those handlebars. I choose the latter, because I am a father. Immediately I realize I have overlooked the downside risk of this second option, which in fact materializes now: the bicycle's underworks barge into my right leg, the chain wheel bites into the shin, and the serrated metal leaves a wound that gapes wide under a grinning flap of flesh. I probably need stitches. I tape the thing instead. I tell Peter I'll bear the scar forever as a reminder of the time he ran his father over. "You mean the first time I ran my father over," he says. Is this idle smartassery? Or genuine threat? I don't know. But I have recorded it here, for public dissemination, in case the latter and I cannot give witness. The scar—I still have it—is the shape of a letter *J*. Part of me sees it on its side and imagines it is a graph showing the necessarily dwindling number of memories I'll make with my son over time. (Look, here's where he leaves for college. And that point there—that's where he gets the job in Guangzhou.) More often I see it upright. More often I decide it stands for joy. |

This Year	He clears my height by a third of a foot.
	He likes to lift his mother one-armed and carry
	her through the house. If his wrists are
	two-by-fours, then mine too, if there were
	a candy bar marketed under the name Two By Four.
	I still give him options, sure, every weekend.
	Lately, they are limited to Xbox or chess.

Dead Now

(1)

THE OLDER COUPLE ON MAPLE STREET WHO LIVED between our house and the Exxon, back in that difficult and sweaty decade when the stauncher folk who said *filling station* had not yet seen their rout by the nulls and dissolutes who favored *gas station*, in a tall blond house with a long blond dog named Blondie and, formerly, with a reportedly beautiful blond daughter named Lisa that according to the block's stoop-sitters got mixed up with drugs in her late teens, and with a fatal overdose before she reached thirty, which is why I never set eyes on her; who let me pet Blondie whenever I happened by; who liked to say as I pet her, "She just loves children, yes, she really is good with kids"; who may have been — though it's impossible to say, which is to say there can be no doubt they were — thinking of, and pining for, and hurting over their own daughter each time they said it: they must be dead now.

(2)

The woman who screamed accented profanities out her third-story window each time I pedaled past her house on my Big Wheel, fat plastic cartoon tires scraping hideously against New Jersey concrete, and it was easy and indeed satisfying to simply scrape away and rumble on without even acknowledging her, as each time I heard her I was already on my way past, which, when you think about it, was maybe the best possible lesson for a second-grader on weathering the assaults of the life to come—i.e., Look Down, Scrape Away, Rumble On: she must be dead now.

(3)

The man with hair over his ears who wore his body concavely, back in that sweaty and difficult decade when a stoop could be impressive, whom our school paid to drive us home in a station wagon, who liked to joke with the oldest and cockiest of the boys—the thirteen-year-olds—and strived at looking as relaxed as they seemed and grinned his way through validating high-fives and lapped up the nicknames and gamely dispensed cigarettes when asked and radiated a peculiar cool-boy mix of boisterousness and breeziness because it compensated for some fracture in his own childhood and perhaps for that reason said nothing and kept on driving like he'd heard nothing when in the rear area of the station wagon the cockiest of these boys told Prajit, Let's go, and now in retrospect knowing what I know about being in vehicles and about driving vehicles and about life in general there was no way the man with hair over his ears could not have heard, and remembering what I remember there was no way this was the first time, because six-year-old Prajit knew immediately what was expected and, still more tellingly, stalled like he hadn't heard, and the boy said, Hey, let's go and You're not fooling anybody and Prajit took his pants down and showed it and the boy said Go ahead, do it and Prajit didn't do anything and

the boy said, Do it, we want to see and Prajit
rolled back the foreskin of his uncircumcised penis and simply waited, on display there, the im-
perious boy fixing a contradictory stare, low lids
all indifference but focus and duration quite the
opposite, and finally breaking off and punching
one hand with the other like he'd solved a good
mystery and launching without anything more
into a new conversation with the other older
boy and turning his back on Prajit who rocked
forward from a squat onto his knees and wrig-
gled up his pants and, hoping to conceal his
humiliation, turned from cowed to furious and
screamed for contrived reasons at Arthur our
little Filipino classmate who in addition to being very little was very kind and it is impossible to know how at age six I saw right through
Prajit's pretense at anger with Arthur to cover
for his shame but failed to see right through the
concave-bodied driver's pretense at not hearing
when he must have heard, and who knows if
he was covering for something in his own past
along the very lines of what he'd gathered was
happening to Prajit, or if maybe he hated Prajit
for it, for reminding him of the weakling he once
was and for making him a weakling again, there
at the steering wheel: he, regrettably, may not be
dead now.

(4)

    The stranger with dyed black hair, frontage
scrupulously combed and shellacked into a kind
of virile bosom, who stopped me poolside at the
community center and pointed at my swimsuit
and on it the blue-and-orange New York Mets
patch that my mother with characteristic immi-

grant cunning had sewn there to equip her son
with some alibi for the fabric's otherwise unac-
ceptable hue of orange (Different-colored swimsuit = dollars. New patch = cents.), said You
like the Mets? and, when he heard Yes from a
boy who could not have named a single player
and with characteristic first-generation self-con-
sciousness spoke the word Yes without conviction (though, in fairness, an alibi for an alibi never made anybody cocksure), said I hope you're a
better swimmer than they are a team and, after
saying this, didn't move from where he stood,
but didn't look at me either, and instead looked
here and looked there as if he were on a mission
to tell the truth wherever truth needed telling:
he must be dead now.

(5)

The ragged-breathing fellow to my imme-
diate right at the counter in a Manhattan location of Chock full o' Nuts, where my parents
and I stopped for a donut one afternoon, who
with an air of consummate routine sipped his
coffee and spread pats of butter onto the slices
of American cheese in front of him and solemnly ate these slices of buttered-processed with a
fork like it was meatloaf, loosing in me an elec-
tric revulsion and also, simultaneously, a reeling
bewilderment at why two things so similar, so
closely derived, but still nonidentical, should together be so loathsome, and did not know that
at this biochemical watershed moment he was
causing my youngster's mind to seize with the
potent oddity of CloseButNotQuiteness — things
akin but still unsame, approxidentities, bow-
tied twins in somber sepia portrait but here the

pinpoint of a shadow tells that one and only one
has the start of a bleeding nose — and who to this
day is responsible for my abhorrence of those
hard white things in hard white light called
hospitals, my preoccupation with almost-Amer-
ica Canada squashed belly-to-back against ex-
tremely-America America, my fascination with
Joyce's snow falling in ocean and Roy's banana
jam and Tolstoy's butler with his fat bright
gleaming face and starched bright gleaming tie,
my unhinged contempt for the successive vowels in Gaelic words and the redundant sauces in
Venezuelan dishes and the compound dysfunc-
tions of self-regarding humorless persons, and
did not know when he turned to me and asked,
"What are you looking at?" that even decades
later I would not know how to answer: he must
be dead now.

(6)

The realization in my late twenties that youth
had been a time of promise, and that aging was
the death of that promise, and that life owed me
nothing; and the realization in my thirties that
this earlier realization had itself been a foolishness of youth, a nice illusion, because youth in
truth had never been a time of promise, but was
merely a front-loaded reprieve, a fleeting sanc-
tuary from the cold wash of existence — lonely,
pointless, futile, dilapidating, and relentless;
these realizations that seemed ridiculous as my
forties pressed against me their musty wool, because it was then I realized that both realizations
had been youthful mistake, that youth was neither promise nor reprieve and both had been nice
illusions, that even when I'd been thinking like

an older person, about how youth was promise extinguished, and even when I'd been thinking that I was thinking like an older person, about how youth was mere reprieve, I'd been a young fool, because life and the world are indifferent, and I and you are bits of material that catch fire for a time and that's all, and when I was young I took youth seriously and thought it was promise and when I was aging I took aging personally and thought it was disappointment, and later as I became what I thought was aged, I apprehended what I thought was the truth: nothing is fundamental, nothing is personal, existence and meaning are names we put on things that do not have us especially in mind, and in the end all is more or less nothing and nothing everything, and we proceed unto death no matter what, and no matter that, we think: both illusions are dead now.

(7)

That weakling version of me that at age six does nothing to help his not best but still pretty good friend Prajit and in fact leers on with the others, which is approxidentical to inflicting, and I remember everything, everything, except why I didn't do something, whether it was because I feared an eighth-grader powerful enough to make sidekicks out of grown-ups or because I — baptized and raised Greek Orthodox, a faith that teaches Christ represents a new covenant upending the need to snip penises and sacrifice oxen, but admittedly in all likelihood condemns one to hell for the view that people are only bits of material that catch fire for a time — was at the time thinking to myself There but for the grace

of Vishnu and Christ Pantocrator go wretchedly
I. But oh I hope it is. Dead now, I mean.

(8)

The eightysomething who come eleven every night made halting way, peering down with
blue-hot intensity, as if silently christening each
of his steps with a different name before taking it, into the Wendy's on Queens Boulevard
where I'd bring my laptop because the dining
room stayed open until two in the morning,
me and the AARP night owls with the place to
ourselves; and the loud eightysomething who
called to the puttering eightysomething from a
booth of autumn-hued propylene, What do you
want? I'll buy it for you. You doing a coffee or
a meal? I'll get you one of these days, not because he owed his puttering friend a coffee or a
meal but to the contrary, as he explained loudly to yet another eightysomething with evident
indifference to who might hear, because in fact
he'd picked up a meal for Greased Lightning
weeks ago when the fellow had forgotten his
wallet at home and because (interrupting himself here to call out again over his shoulder, I
got to get you one of these days!) it was against
moral code to dun a debt so small, so instead he
was hectoring the fellow with offers of generosity to prod him into remembering the debt and
paying it back—thus proving, without prejudice
to the separate question of who the bigger shit
might have been in this scenario, the truth that
people even when they're eightysomething can
be real shits: they, all of them, must be dead now.

(9)

The man who shouted "Use the bathroom!" across ShopRite's parking lot when he spotted my father, Greek-born and raised in a mule-track village, standing at the edge of the pavement urinating onto a clump of weeds and who—after my father put up a conciliatory hand and ineffectually, incongruently, humiliatingly responded by lofting the mere word "Yes?" and after his son inside the car winced from embarrassment because his son was too young to know Rumbling On when he heard it—purported to know from one little syllable across an asphalt expanse what my father was about and how to stab the kid in the back seat where it hurt and shouted again, "In this country we use the bathroom!": he must be dead now.

(10)

The blind man tasked by the municipality to gather up eggs for reuse after the Easter egg hunt at the town park at Palisade and 24th who approached my mother and sister and me and asked for our plastic eggs and was refused by my mother with a rather grim definitiveness and then explained he wasn't asking for the candy back, only the egg containers themselves once emptied of candy, and then it was my mother's turn to explain, provoked into ferocity by some atavistic hypersensitivity to threats against offspring, that he was mistaken if he thought he should be collecting hard-earned eggs from children after an Easter egg hunt and moreover should be ashamed of himself for trying, and the blind man who didn't know what to do just stood there with his hands in front of his waist,

thumbs nursing a litter of shy fingers, and finally turned around — he could have shrugged, it
seemed to me, but didn't — and walked off without a trace of rancor, leaving me in a spiny welter
of confusions that, here I am a full-grown man
and gray hair to boot, I still haven't worked out,
leaving me to wonder for decades why they'd
send a blind man to collect Easter eggs when the
foundational premise of an Easter egg hunt was
the challenge in gathering them, indeed for children whose eyes were closer to the ground and,
moreover, functioning, and to feel guilt that I
might think of a blind man as ineligible to collect
Easter eggs, and to resent my mother for yelling at a blind man who was just doing his job,
and to give thanks for a mother who would yell
for me even at a blind man doing his job, and to
resent the blind man for creating a foreseeably
untenable situation in which I might end up re-
senting my mother, and I do not remember how
the candy tasted but I do savor the memory so
well that though in the Greek Orthodox faith the
tradition on Easter morning is to approach one
another and say Christ is risen and Indeed he is
risen I think to say instead Long ago on this day,
my beautiful mother, cruel with love and sweet,
prevailed against a blind man: he must be dead
now.

(11)

The notion that all is more or less nothing
when even a stumbling encounter with a pure
stranger can change the bent of a mind and the
sense of a life, when even dumbest happenstance has consequence, has in fact a brunt and
fervor that can outstrip all we know and outlast

even our deaths: that, I realize—sure took long
enough—is foolishness.

(12)
    And dead now.

Tampa, Florida, 1184 B.C.

MY MOTHER IS CUBAN, A RETIRED SCHOOLTEACHER. My father is Greek, a former oil tanker captain and sandwich shop owner. We moved from Weehawken to Tampa when I was nine. My father couldn't take another winter. "This cold is to hell," he used to complain.

In Tampa I was enrolled at a certain long-established, church-affiliated school. It was where the rich kids went. We could afford it only because the church had a boys' choir that offered school scholarships to good singers, and puberty had not yet changed my voice into the mediocrity it is today.

This new school was a shock.

I was the only kid from the North. Every time I asked to use the bathroom Ms. Parsons in penmanship retorted there was none and I would not fit in the sink no matter how I tried. "You mean the *restroom*, Mister Choundas."

I was one of a very few children at the school with immigrant parents. The first time our homeroom teacher Ms. Drindy left the classroom, I watched the other ethnic kid—Matt Arenas—pop out of his seat and plead with K.J. Cantor before K.J. calmly, almost dutifully, kicked Matt's groveling body up and down each aisle of the classroom. The boy in front of me caught my look of horror and explained, apparently to reassure, "They do this all the time."

And I was not rich. At all. School got out at 3:13. I perched every afternoon on the waist-high walls that bracketed the school's entrance not to get picked up but to watch the other children board all manner of gleaming automobilia, including two DeLoreans, and triumph away. Both my parents worked. When my ride came it was at 5 p.m. and in the form of my mother's 1976 Chevrolet Nova. That car's blue was so dull you could persuade yourself they'd forgotten the topcoat and it was primer you were looking at.

My salvation was Homer. The *Iliad.* Richmond Lattimore's translation. This was what Ms. Drindy's class was reading when I arrived at the school in January of 1982.

Thank God for the *Iliad.*

The class was on Book 9. I read Books 1–8 on my own to catch up. Maybe this was what sparked my love? The fact I was lighting through the story alone, with urgency, and not plodding ground in the company of reluctant classmates?

Definitely. But so much more.

I was a former public school kid, now swamped with an average of six hours — *six hours* — of homework a night. But what did this matter when a whole army of grown men, across a sea from home, were seating their molars and standing their ground and getting their arms lopped off and their guts extricated for it? What did this matter when some bit of those six hours got to be spent in their company?

A dismaying proportion of my classmates were weird and abusive and precocious in a bad way. (Tillie Ford in her Add-a-Bead necklace liked to spread sex rumors about classmates with a smiling, elfin cheer. Paul McCrorie was often asked breezily what he and his father were doing that weekend; it was widely known his father had run out on the family years earlier.) But they too had read Books 1–8. And when they learned I was Greek, I was no longer the odd bespectacled child who referred awkwardly to "soda" and "tissues" rather than "Coke" and "Kleenex." They gave me the benefit of the doubt. I was descended from heroes.

The teachers were fantastically strict. Some hung paddles on their walls — as much to ensure ready access as to deter — but paddling was for mere misdemeanors. Serious malfeasances were cause for referral to the mutton-chopped headmaster, whose canings of tender palms were so notorious that every child at the school, caned or not, knew that follow-through actually lessens the pain while flicking back immediately upon impact somehow explodes it by orders of fuckingchristitude. But canings and paddlings were trivial. Teachers, headmaster: immaterial. I was Diomedes.

When we ran out onto the outdoor deck for recess right after Literature, still sopping with Homer, every boy would call out who he wanted to be — proud Hector, hoss-in-chief Agamemnon, clever Odysseus. I claimed the same hero every time: Diomedes. Not Achilles, the finest warrior, or Ajax, the strongest specimen. I was Diomedes: reliable, steadfast, a one-man army. I was Diomedes, who demanded no honors and claimed no glory, but just put his head down and prevailed, who moved through the ranks of Trojans like a spinning axe, who breezily ignored K.J. Cantor's short and mischievous sidekick Andy Hollett (it appears every bully gets one assigned) and Andy's signature random slide tackles out of nowhere, who after stepping inadvertently on a patch of grass while running during gym class through Old Hyde Park under Coach Calhoun's unfailing gaze wrote on control-ruled paper "I will not step on the grass" 499 out of 500 times but "I will yet step on the grass" at line 435 (Suck it, Calhoun), who reveled in victory after crying from his only caning because he stopped crying quickly enough that no one saw.

I look back on those days, and I puzzle over how I drew strength, in such a very real way, from a handful of chapters about the son of Tydeus, dead for three millennia. On the one hand, it was inescapably childish. I lived the clothbound version of mindless superhero envy. On the other hand, it was winsome in a way, and by this I mean it maybe showed, implausibly, a bit of maturity I do not remember having. Because, at bottom, Diomedes's only virtue was persistence. Without recourse to any conviction in his own superiority. Without the justification of any obvious outward exceptionalism. Pure, willed persistence. And I marvel that at age ten I had the capacity—and the desperation, for fair—to learn that this least colorful and most workmanlike of all qualities was the realest superpower there is.

—

Glory, Finally, at the Parker House

—

Art knows no death like a waking child.
— ANONYMOUS

(Okay, not anonymous. I wrote
it. I had to, because it hadn't been
written before, and even chances
that's because all the authors in
history on the brink of the same
formulation were prevented from
it by a waking child.)

WRITING IS A STRUGGLE. EVERYBODY KNOWS THAT. It is hard to do, and exceedingly hard to do well, yet recognition is rare and fleeting. Glory is nonexistent. Friends comprehend little of what we do and why we do it. Relatives do not even ask. There are no parades for writers.

Children: also a struggle. Everybody knows that. Not even children like the idea of having their own children. Just ask them to paint your room or drive you to the park and they stare like you're the unreasonable one.

Writers with children: these reside in a quadruple hell. Specifically:

There are the twin hells of writing and children. Now, I love my kids with an ache. Equally important, I *like* them, too. They are kind and fascinating and make excellent company. They are also a total pain in the ass.

There is the third hell of mutual preclusion. Each of writing and children prevents the full pursuit and enjoyment of the other. They leave intact each other's downsides of stress and obligation, but kick out of reach the joyous upsides of immersive wonder and iterative venturing. Take children.[1] They are a life-jacking. They make impossible such frivolities as showering, and eating from plates, and writing nice things to read. Writing, for its part, knows how to stick it to children. Writing is a heady isolation that, for a parent, comes only by thieving time and would-be memories from one's own spawn. How many of my stories turned dark and furtive and captious because I wrote them with the cagey desperation of a stowaway, sleep-deprived and under constant threat of discovery? Indeed, how much of the spleen in this very paragraph results from my seven-year-old daughter having awoken at six this very morning to come down to the kitchen and tell me with great urgency that Grandpa not only ate one of the donuts she made from the Japanese candy design kit I brought home for her from H-Mart but also agreed with her that chocolate-with-strawberry-sauce was best (thus not simply interrupting my writing but leaving me wondering distractedly, long after she'd toddled out of the kitchen, how Grandpa could have responsibly come to such a conclusion if he'd sampled only the one donut)?

There is the fourth hell of mutual evocation. Children are mobile concentrates of what we most like to write about. They are innocent and psychotic and brazen and bizarre and unrelenting and swollen with feeling and new. It is impossible to spend an hour with a child and not see or hear something that makes you want to remember it forever—which is to say, to write it down. You tear yourself away from

---

[1] Please. (Henny Youngman had two children. Relatedly, he is known for having written ten thousand one-liners, not fifty thousand five-liners.)

the kid and sit down to write in the hard-won hush of a closed room and take gemütlich-grade pleasure in nesting your finger pads just right in the demure concavities of *asdf* and *jkl*, and after only a minute you think, *Why can't I just hang out a little more with [name of child]?* Writing is lonely and intricate and involuted. Children are chirpy and giggly and full of farts. You shut the laptop and open the door and the moment you smell the grape juice and see the unhinged look that says, "You are mine now, all mine, and nobody nobody nobody talks more SPILLS MORE SCREAMS MORE," it occurs to you how agreeably the keys of a laptop shwist down and lottle around and plap back up for more and how rarely they leak mucus, and you find yourself edging your way out of the room, thinking, *Slowly, but slowly, because running will just provoke it.*

The frankest conflict between children and writing may be the early morning wake-up. There are a hundred reasons to wake up early to write, and the top three alone are compelling: the mind is fresh and unjaded by the day's experience; the residual haze of sleep disables self-censoring inhibitions; the practice of writing before doing anything else reinforces for the subconscious mind its priority significance. But young children are allergic with an oppressive specificity to the sounds of a writer getting out of bed. I try to wake up at 5:13 every morning (an arbitrary and memorably specific hour that is difficult to cheat past or ignore) but never do I dress immediately. My house was built in 1898. Putting on clothes in the bedroom would mean a symphony of creaking floorboards and, soon thereafter, a coda of two caterwauling kids from down the hall. ("Daddy! Daaaaaaaaaaaaaaaaaa aaaaaaaaaaaaaaaaaaaaaaaaaaaaaaaaaaaaaaaaaaaa aaaaaaaaaaaaaaaaaaaaaaaaaaaaaaaaaaaaaady!") Instead I creep down the stairs in my boxers, carrying shoes and socks and pants and shirt and the tatters of dignity shredded by expediency, and dress myself in the kitchen. The linoleum licks my bare feet like an eager, frigid, dehydrated dog. This, I think to myself—staring outside into the predawn murk and misbuttoning my shirt into a parallelogram (three windows means I must dress in the dark)—is the writing life.

Vacation only escalates the conflict. You board the plane or pack the car with risible visions of unbounded time and sovereignty. Vacation, after all, used to mean you do what you want. But that was before children. Vacation *with* children means guarding prisoners without the benefit of a prison. "Doing what you want" becomes a Zen koan, appealing in a far-off, incomprehensible way. Writing in the mornings turns into a mad scientist's foam of complications. At 5:13 a.m., you find yourself in a hotel room. Whereas normally you fumble for your clothing and laptop in familiar surroundings, here you do so without remembering the layout. You are stealthy as an elk. Whereas normally an intervening wall affords you some margin of error, here in a snug room the bittiest sound works instant and massive catastrophe. You are quiet as a jewel thief if by "jewel thief" one means an elk. And there is nothing to be done with a hotel room door that makes so gratuitously sonorous a bank-vault noise that clearly it has been engineered by some wry, lurking intelligence for the purpose of mocking you and this elk-burglar campaign of yours.

What then? You abscond to a common area in the hotel that shows no hospitality to the hungry, thirsty, and uncaffeinated. But abscond you do and find a place to write near the elevator bank in an armchair so lurid with swirl and fleck that the fabric itself is demonstrably worse than any combination of stains its havoc was presumably calculated to conceal, or in a stray hard-backed chair outside the second-floor conference rooms where a security guard will spy you in the camera and come a-lumbering in six-point-five minutes to demand with all the gruffness he can contrive to examine your room key, or on a couch in the lobby that cannot be quiet because at that small intimate hour the sparse staff call to each other at a proprietary and often startling volume.

These, then, were the challenges when one August I ventured with my wife and two children to Boston for a kind of family reunion. We met my parents there, as well as my sister and her husband and their two kids. My sister is a person who will email you within forty-eight hours of publication a copy of an obituary from a neighborhood newspaper announcing the untimely death of the salutatorian from your graduating high school class, this neighborhood newspaper being *published abroad* in a language that neither you nor she speaks. My sister has a normal office — I know this because I've seen it in person — but nevertheless I always imagine her enthroned in a gamer's infini- featured leather chair wearing an earpiece, infrared goggles, and a miner's headlamp,[2] swiveling grimly

---

[2] Why would she need a headlamp if she's got infrared? you ask. I answer, Do not try me. My daughter woke up at six this morning to talk Japanese candy.

before a curving bank of blinking consoles and flashing monitors that survey a planet's worth of information every few seconds, and paying no mind to the drop of blood beading in the corner of her left eye from the violence with which her frontal lobe processes it all. No surprise, therefore, when she found rooms at the Parker House in Boston for under $200 a night.

Now, please appreciate that my family is not a luxury-hotel-type family. We stay in Red Roofs and Comfort Inns, and Hampton Inns if we're feeling fancy. Two hundred dollars might be the budget for an entire trip, not a night. On the other hand, a family reunion is something special, and so is the Parker House. It is the longest continuously operating hotel in the United States. It is where the Parker House roll and the Boston cream pie were invented. It is where Ho Chi Minh worked as a baker and Malcolm X as a busboy, where John F. Kennedy proposed to Jackie Bouvier and announced his candidacy for Congress.

It also happens to be a storied place for writers. Charles Dickens lived for a time in Room 520. Apparently he did his first reading of *A Christmas Carol* there. A group calling themselves the Saturday Club met at the hotel every Saturday. Its members included some people named Ralph Waldo Emerson, Henry Wadsworth Longfellow, and Nathaniel Hawthorne.

I wonder whether those accomplished writers had a motto or a mission statement of some kind. Generally speaking, I do not go in for slogans or creeds. But the writing life, at least for me, requires a very self-conscious, overtly imposed kind of discipline, and the following principle has helped me enormously:

Write every day. Write every single day. Except when you're sick or on vacation, in which case write every day while sick or on vacation.

So even in Boston—on vacation, in beautiful sunny August, my parents on the cusp of their forty-fifth wedding anniversary—I stick to the regimen. The first morning, I wake up in Room 614 at 5:13 a.m. I exit the room barefoot, carrying under my left arm a shirt and pants and socks and shoes and over my right shoulder a laptop bag. I wear only an undershirt and boxers. What does it matter what I'm wearing? Who at a luxury hotel in August goes abroad at 5:13 a.m.? Could they blame me if they knew the scope and power of the human detonation that my idiosyncratic measures were averting? These are the reassuring indignations I feed myself, but precautions are taken nonetheless: I head away from the elevators toward an end-piece of corridor that turns a corner. It is a dead-end stub of a hallway, with only a couple of doors off each side, and so a good place for avoiding observation while dressing. Hurriedly I throw on my clothes and then backtrack to the elevators. My destination choices are the lobby, a sprawling space with desk-height round tables and plentiful chairs, and the mezzanine, a dim place with hallway nooks and plump couches and coffee tables. Both are sweet writing spots. The mezzanine is empty of people. The lobby contains only a few hotel staff, and they are sufficiently morning-giddy and mutually absorbed that none of them notices me. On this first morning, I choose both, starting in the mezzanine and then—for a change of pace—moving to the lobby. Great success. I reap more than a few tasty sentences.

The second morning, I wake up and grab my usual items and haul ajar the implausibly dense slab of dungeon-cured dragon's tooth they've installed for a hotel-room door and then, stepping into the corridor and swiveling around, guide this monstrosity back into its frame of Jupiter-mined ore. The more racket this door makes, the more in a hurry I am to close it, and thus the more racket it makes. I learned these facts on Morning #1 — moreover the fact that whispering "Fucking hell" at a door does little to quiet it — but my adaptive intelligence is such that both dismal performance and profane voiceover on Morning #2 are unchanged.

The door shuts and I turn around. There's a man standing there, watching me. It's a maintenance guy. He's down the corridor, closer to the elevator bank than to my room. His body cants a little toward the elevators, suggesting that the sight of me, a caricature of a half-dressed man escaping a hotel room, has frozen him in position. He's grinning and nodding his head. I think to offer something — a greeting, an explanation — but I can't, because the necessary volume to make myself heard would risk stirring the hive I've just escaped so excruciatingly. Finally he turns and strolls off, no longer regarding me but still nodding his head, presses a button on the wall, turns to take me in for another moment, and then — just before disappearing into an elevator — gives me a sharp little salute.

Whatever. I slink the opposite way to my plush-carpeted bolt-hole, get dressed, and take an elevator down to the lobby. The doors part. I emerge into the lobby. This is what I hear: "There he is."

Around me shine a ring of faces, most of

them familiar from previous lobby transits but
entirely different now for being trained in my
direction: the slender gentleman who I suspect
is older than his baby-face looks suggest, the
still older fellow with the bearing and haircut
of former military or law enforcement, the short
one in his thirties who works with another so
similar-looking they must constantly be taken
for brothers, the front-desk clerk barely out of
college. Their eyes are wide and shining, their
grins are wild, and they're gazing at me delight-
edly, even expectantly. I stop, wondering what
they're about. And then I see the maintenance
guy standing among them, wearing the biggest
grin of all. The picture resolves. Mister Maintenance is the advance scout who has brought
news from the sixth floor of an absconding lover making his desperate, ridiculous, heroic get-
away. The resulting scene is a miniature of what
I imagine Charles Lindbergh experienced on de-
planing in France. I give them a little chest-high
wave and proceed toward the far portion of the
lobby. Along the way they insist on paying me
hearty respects in serial fashion: "Nicely done,
my friend." "You in and you out." Somebody
says a third thing, and it sounds like, "Who the
ninja?" One of their number hangs back in silent
admiration.

Do I consider righting their misapprehen-
sion? Yes. But I don't. I am exhausted by the
mere contemplation of the joyless and wandering exposition that would be needed to clarify
my circumstances. Instead, I grin wider than
they do and I take their congratulations as they
are offered and I report to the farthest table
down the length of the lobby to start my writing.
The reality of what's happening here isn't lost on

me: these are workers harnessed into mundane routines. Sure, they are upbeat and amiable. Yes, they shwist down and lottle around and plap back up for all they're worth. But they are at that gray and hard thing called work. And they are thrilled by the prospect that something different, unexpected, and (that gold standard of workaday life) *worth a retelling* might present itself this random morning. We all want the myth to happen. All of us — the concierges in their key-adorned blazers, the writers in their Danimals-stained khakis — want life to be bigger.

So I do the same thing. I take this little misunderstanding and I turn it to my own purposes and I make the myth happen. I decide my crowd of admirers was welcoming and nurturing and celebrating not the lover of 614 but the writer of 5:13. I decide every felicitation lavished in the past few moments was a trophy for keeping true to my craft. "Nicely done," indeed, whenever a writer climbs out of bed to write. "You in and you out," of course, because the heart of each scene must be carved rough and presented bloody, and the sentences rendered with all the grit and dispatch a lack of caffeine will allow. And ninjahood — an infinite capacity in all us coarse, fumbling mortals for magic and for greatness — was perhaps what they had in mind when Dickens wrote that dreams "sport on earth in the night season," and Hawthorne that life is "marble and mud," and Louisa May Alcott that "I want to be great, or nothing," and Danielle Legros Georges that "In spite of all who would renounce petals / the petals come."

I open my laptop a little before half-past-five that morning in August, and I decide there are parades for writers.

Nothing Like a Pandemic

I TEACH CLAIRE CHESS. SHE'S NINE. AFTER EXAMPLE moves, and a few trial runs, we play a full game. I don't give 100 percent. I don't roll over, either. I play half-assed. I consider all available moves but not all their implications.

I am shocked when she beats me. She makes at least one critical move I fail to anticipate. In my book that's a solid win.

Still, she refuses to call the knight a knight. She calls it a horse. This only amplifies her victory. It's like losing a tennis match to someone who calls her racket a thingie.

We FaceTime Peter's and Claire's grandparents. The result is that weird mix of generations where the grandparents can't hear and the grandchildren irreverently suggest the ensuing non sequiturs are drug-related.

CLAIRE: Grandma, we're making peanut butter cookies with M&Ms!

GRANDMA: You're making M&Ms?!

PETER: Grandma, how are we going to make M&Ms? Are you smoking the weed again?

GRANDMA: Am I what?

PETER: Are you smoking the weed?

GRANDMA: Am I smoking the what?

PETER: The weeeeed. Grandma, the weed.

GRANDMA: Peter, are your bros leaving you alone?

PETER: Yes. They're in quarantine.

GRANDMA: Are they home?

PETER: Yes, Grandma, they're in quarantine. Where are they going to be? Grandma, are you okay? Did you find my stash, Grandma?

GRANDMA: Did I what?

PETER: Are you weeding the smoke, Grandma?

Peter is a good boy. But he's fourteen. And if it sounds like I'm suggesting that's the opposite of good, then we understand each other. The next thing that happens during this FaceTime is: Peter moons my father-in-law. This being Peter's grandfather, they share the kind of utterly insular and on-its-own-terms relationship that renders moot, ridiculous, all outside judgment. Knowing my place here, I say nothing. Peter positions the phone with a deliberate hand and, with the other, slips his pants off his ass. The phone screen fills with underwear.

Peter's grandfather watches this. He's open-mouth laughing. Couldn't be more delighted. Now, Bill has cerebral palsy. Reciprocating with his own moon would involve incremental movements requiring outsized time and effort. On the other hand, Bill is half-Irish and half-Scot. Have you seen *Braveheart*?

Forty-five seconds later—belts can be complicated—Peter is staring wide-eyed at his grandfather's underwear. Nothing like a pandemic to turn a bluff teenager into a giggler.

After dinner, Claire demands we play chess a second time. "I don't know if this makes sense," she says, "or if it's grammatically correct. But I *do* know *you* will know so hard I'm beating you that the knowing will hurt." I understand exactly what she's saying. It's the most potent trash talk I've heard in years.

Again she beats me. Now she's calling the knights "cow things." I'm fairly certain this is pure provocation.

The family goes for an outdoor walk. We pass people at a remove. Twice we encounter friends. It's hard to keep six feet away and not seem stinting and self-involved and supercilious. It's hard to smile from six feet away and not feel sure others suspect pretense in that smile. On the way home, we talk how at least the virus will give us new experiences, irrevocable memories.

A half-hour later, Claire and I drive to Key Food. We're wearing face masks. She pipes up from the back seat.

CLAIRE: First time going out in a mask.

GEORGE: Yeah.

CLAIRE: We were talking about making memories.

GEORGE: Yeah.

CLAIRE: This is definitely a memory.

GEORGE: Yeah.

CLAIRE: We'll never forget this.

GEORGE: Yeah.

Claire and I split the shopping list. By maximizing efficiency, we will minimize in-store time and, thus, the risk of exposure. I'm getting milk, yogurt, dumplings, and frozen pizza. Claire's in charge of SourPatch Kids, Hershey's Kisses, and Reese's Mini Peanut Butter Cups. One of us has the better assignment.

On the ride home, Claire pipes up from the back seat.

CLAIRE: People were staring at me.

GEORGE: 'Cause you're wearing a mask.

CLAIRE: Not just that.

GEORGE: What?

CLAIRE: Because I'm a kid in the candy aisle. I'm a kid wearing a mask in the candy aisle.

GEORGE: So?

CLAIRE: Like a kid in a candy store.

GEORGE: Oh. Like you should be all happy, but then you're wearing a plague mask.

CLAIRE: Yup.

GEORGE: Huh.

Self-awareness. Scrutiny of motivation. Knowledge of the dark fur that can cling to the ordinary.

Nothing like a pandemic to turn a nine-year-old into a sage.

—

My Muse is Gaffay

—

SOME MORNINGS, THE SUN LOOKS WRONG OUTSIDE my window. I sit at the kitchen table shaking salt into the hairs on my arm, and a feeling shoves up in me: It's finished. Everything went past, without me." Jennifer Egan, *A Visit from the Goon Squad*.

I saw those lines and I was like, "Whoa." But Egan, she didn't care.

"As Khubchand lay dying on his cushion, Estha could see the bedroom window reflected in his smooth, purple balls. And the sky beyond. And once a bird that flew across." Arundhati Roy, *The God of Small Things*.

I remember where and how I was sitting when I first read those sentences. But do you think that mattered to Roy?

"Eventually, as his meat and his clothes went away into the air and his foot bones slipped their loose nooses, he relaxed into a dignified cuddle around the stake and in the hole. He had planted himself and it was a nice job." G. K. Wuori, "Angles," *Nude in Tub*.

Gobsmacked. That's what I was. I was gobsmacked by this paragraph. But Wuori paid me no mind.

Great writing, so far as I can tell, just doesn't care. It concerns itself with nothing except what it's about. It cuts where a cut is needed. It is headlong, and insolent, and minerally indifferent to

expectation. Writers and great writers are
pleased to have their work admired, sure, same
as the next freak. But let me tell you, when
they're in the act of great writing? They disdain
admiration and its prospect both.

There's a phrase for exactly this mix of boldness and indignation. I know because I've spent
my entire professional life in New York. *I could
give a fuck,* is what you say. Magically, instantly,
the attitude is summoned. Not a rat's ass or a
good goddamn, mind, because this isn't cotillion
with Grandma. Neither a crap nor a shit. A fuck.
The sure-mindedness registered is maximum.

Sometimes the writer on the bucking hump
of great writing catches himself thinking, "But
what will They think?" For this eventuality there
is but a single protocol: (1) Grab mane with one
hand and, with other, ram fist in Their mouth,
holding it there, elbow-deep in slick esophagus.
(2) Rear back, you and your unbiddable prose,
until all you see is sky.

There is a phrase for exactly this mix of indignation and boldness. I know because I grew up
in Florida and went to school in Georgia. *Fuck all
y'all,* is what you say, and instantly, magically,
the sentiment is secured. Doesn't matter if one
soul or twenty, or none, loiter within earshot.
Now it's you against the world.

Have you ever seen a great actor? A truly
great actor, on the stage, in the flesh? There's a
scorn that comes off her in waves and we can
feel it there in the seats. She doesn't cater, she
doesn't sneak looks to see if it's working. She is
pure venture, pure undertaking, and unavail-
able to anything other than the enterprise itself.

There's an implicit scorn for the audience — that's what the fourth wall really is, it's a wonderful scorn — because she's due somewhere and we're the late hour and the trees blurring past.

I haven't mastered the secret to great writing. But I've written it down. Here it is:

My muse is a Frenchman, his name is Gaffay.
From him I learned how to write and what to say.
G-A-F is for Give a fuck,
F-A-Y is for Fuck all y'all.
There is no way, none, except mine is the way.

You have questions. Why don't the middle lines rhyme? you wonder. How is it that Gaffay, a Frenchman, shows such facility with regional American slang?

The answer to these questions and others — and I think I've covered this — is that I could give a fuck, so fuck all y'all.

In the Covidium

PLEASANTVILLE, NEW YORK

Day P. Since the stay-at-home order we shower mostly in the evenings. After tonight's shower I put on cologne for the do of it. It's gone rancid. Top notes of rusted sled runner, base notes of a fat fruit left to roll under the hot working parts of a grocery cooler and abandoned there.

Each day the same as the next. Turns out it's refreshing novelty, a surprise rot.

Day P + 3. When I was young my father sold hot dogs for a living. Occasionally I'd go to work with him, ride in the step van to his spot between the Jersey City Medical Center and the Montgomery Gardens housing complex. I'd watch him make change, and fantasize about eating all the barbecue chips, and ask to see the starter pistol he once showed the customer who showed him a knife. My dad's real name is Panagiotis. He told customers his name was Joe.

I love things with two names. Our parents used to take my sister and me to eat out once a week; the place was called Gino's Kentucky Fried Chicken. All her life my mother told me she dreamed one day of owning a Lincoln Continental, and by the time she finally bought one, at age seventy-four, the model name was no longer

"Lincoln Continental" or "Lincoln Town Car" — but "Lincoln Continental Town Car."

Which is it? *Forget which,* says the double-named object. *Forget being silly. It's both. Double names are for the replete. I am a thing extreme. I am excess and stupendous. So much much needs two names.*

This plague, it ruins even the felicity of a double name. Is it the novel coronavirus? Or COVID-19? The answer is yes. Such does its threat and menace sprawl, so fickly does it choose and so variously does it punish, it needs a second name to fit.

Day P + 7. I have become a person who draws connoisseur distinctions among bleach wipes, palpating admiringly the specimens from the sopping bottom of the can.

Day P + 12. In the course of each rootless, hapless attempt to make sense of it, a dark-web part of my brain posits the answer in glow-green-on-conspiracy-black hypertext. COVID-19 must be Generation X's bill come due for the implausibly golden era of the 1990s. Oil embargoes and gas shortages ended with the 1970s. Fears of Cold War armageddon faded with the 1980s. The 1990s were a victory lap. Peace prevailed, peoples flourished. Historians called it the end of history. Even the coldest eyes saw a unipolar world where America at least tried to be the good guy.

But all in life is a trade-off, and the era of improbable boon dragged behind it the inevitable reversal. The 2001 attacks marred the dream; the

2008 recession mangled it; the 2020 pandemic means to murder it and bury it in nightmare.

We've lost jobs, peace of mind. Loved ones. It is ridiculous, then, to notice that the millennials must choose between beards and a proper mask fit. That the retirees have been dispossessed of their stay-at-home monopoly. That the Genexers watch their cohort generations pay a karma tax they don't rightly owe.

Is the explanation facile? Reductive? Yes. Both are its name. It is excess and stupid. It is the explanation from the sopping bottom of my brain.

Day P + 14. Monday morning. A school day. I'm in the kitchen getting coffee. In comes Claire, nine and hazel-eyed. She's pirouetting and humming lightly to herself. She's not approaching to ask a schoolwork question. She's not going to the fridge or the cabinets for a snack. It's not clear what she's doing.

What are you doing?

Claire looks at me for the first time, still pirouetting.

Twirls, she says, and twirls back out the same way she came.

Of course. Twirls.

Rome, Italy

Day R. My cousin Tania lives in Rome. She is an anesthesiologist by training. In today's Rome, however, all doctors are plague doctors.

At least she is accustomed to masked

patients.

There are a lot of them. Same symptoms, same diagnosis. A hospital full of clones. More even than before, the doctors and the nurses work to remember the patients' personhood, to say their names. They pretend it's not betrayal when death comes so easily, nonchalantly. For their troubles they get obliteration.

Day R + 40. Tania is hospitalized with the coronavirus. Not hospitalized; she's already inside. She is admitted. She trades lanyard for bracelet.

She calls her husband, speaks with both sons. Basically it's a very long shift with a very short patient roster.

She is all the things you'd expect. Hopelorn, subjugated, terrified.

Logic used to be a solace. Now it is a demon. Exposure was always both impossible — every precaution assiduously observed, meticulously administered, glove, mask, gown, mask, shield, mask, mask, mask — and inevitable.

They give her an antimalarial called hydroxy-chloroquine and an antiviral called Kaletra. Eating is out of the question. Thinking about eating sets off waves of revulsion. Acknowledging as a notional matter for even a fleeting moment the proposition that eating food is a thing humans are known to do means plunging into a dark spinning infinite roiling quease.

Day R + 43. Lying in the bed next to Tania's is an old woman. She tells Tania about her life in scattered pieces. She is alert. But speaking more than a few sentences exhausts her. It's up to Tania to put the pieces in order.

Day R + 45. The old woman is not doing well. At night, Tania goes over and caresses the side of the woman's head, brushing lightly through her white hair, thin but so soft. Tania also holds the woman's hand. Now and then the woman squeezes briefly, hard. It's as clear as if she were speaking the words.

Don't leave me.

Day R + 46. The old woman passes away. Tania watches as they put her in a bag, as they zip the bag almost closed, as they spray the inside of the bag, fill the bag with spray, keep spraying, as still they spray even after nobody could doubt there is enough spray. Stop spraying. Looking away is the same as leaving. Tania watches as they lift the bag and gurney it away. The gurney does not clatter; it glides smooth, like everything is just as it should be. The gurney is a liar.

Day R + 48. At the discharge desk, a nurse — a colleague — regards her. She has never seen a look like this before. It is an electrifying mix of warmth and pity and envy and frank delight. He says to her:

You've returned to life.

Tania leaves the hospital, walks home. It is the walk of her life. She is overwhelmed by the kindness of the air. There's so much of it, carrying sun, endless. She cannot repay the air.

Hollywood, California

Day H. In the covidium, every night is Movie Night. My wife, Cathy, and Claire get the couch, Peter the plush red chair. I get the leather chair against the wall.

Blade Runner: People in the future are so tired and tired of things—and there are a lot of things, buzzing and blinking and making people tired—that every sentence or piece of dialogue comes after a pause of between ten and fifteen minutes.

Day H + 2. *Terminator 2:* Things are not what they seem. The clean-cut gentleman wearing a police uniform is a slaughter machine. He's made of liquid, which seems weak, but in fact proves near-invincible.

Day H + 3. *The Blackcoat's Daughter*: Prep school students stuck on campus after the end of the semester start worshipping the furnace in the basement. They kill people, too.

Peter is fourteen and Claire, you know already, is nine. Cathy and I have a working theory that films depicting a reality bleaker than the covidium can't help but be uplifting.

A working theory is not the same as a theory that works.

Day H + 4.
Day H + 5.
Day H + 6. *Titanic*: Three nights. It's a long-ass movie.

It's also a merely sensational movie, made interesting by a single detail.

Jack tells Rose to meet him at the ship's clock and waits—but *facing the clock.* We assume he can't stand the idea she might not come.

Later, as the ship sinks, Mister Andrews, the ship's designer, loiters near the clock in a kind of fugue—paying no attention to the canting decks, the fleeing passengers—*facing the clock.* We assume he's lost his mind.

Still later, the 102-year-old Rose dies peacefully in bed, and in the afterlife that follows—a sequence ecstatic and aglow—the ship's captain and crew and passengers, very much alive, greet her in the Grand Hall with bows and beaming smiles, and there, at the top of the staircase, stands Jack. *Facing the clock.*

The clock, we realize, represents neither desperation nor psychosis. It stands for fate; inevitability; surrender. They face the clock because the everyday around them, the world of sweat and furniture, has fallen away, finally immaterial. The inevitable reigns. Facing the clock is looking away. Looking away is the same as leaving.

The old life cants unrecognizable under our feet. No longer can we contrive significance. No longer can we book appointments to be clamored for, travel to feel indispensable. In the covidium, we face the clocks, the calendars, the news, the phones, the Zooms, the simulacra. The everyday world shrinks away. We cede to the inevitable.

Claire is scandalized at seeing a priceless gem tossed into the ocean. Peter insists he would "rock" Billy Zane, with or without weapons.

Day H + 8. *Matilda*: Nothing bleak about it. We watch it because it's brilliant. There is no villain more terrifying in the history of cinema than Agatha Trunchbull. There is no come-uppance sweeter than telekinesis, deft and restrained. There is no happier ending than living with Miss Honey, second name Bumble-bee, in a well-porched house lush with flowers.

Day H + 10. *Total Recall*: A resistance-fighting-sex-worker type has three breasts. She bares them. She lets a treacherous cab-driver spy fondle them. In fairness, the movie is about a lot of other stuff, too. It's hard to remember what else. The rest of the film I spent thinking, We are either the best parents in the world or the worst.

Day Finally. Here's a film. In the postcovidi-um, we eat food alongside happy strangers. We approach each other with abandon. We while away the day with Miss Honey on the porch, maskless, entertaining streams of hug-grade visitors, backs to all the clocks.

Later, come evening and fireflies, we move to the sloping lawn and dare our visitors to ask.

Twirls, obviously.

The Middle of the Center

Daphne du Maurier called it a prison, Evelyn Waugh a neurosis, and Donna Tartt an ungainly sadness. Philip Roth likened it to the insides of a lion's ear.

Fine writers. About midtown Manhattan they were flat wrong, all of them. These characterizations are as faithful as a jailbreak. They are valuable, however, as empirical proof that the heady, gland-goosing scent that pours from the roasted-nut vending carts known as Nuts 4 Nuts—sweet, hearthish, at once robust and benign—really can blow the brain's fuses.

59th and Lex:

A window designer creeps about a display in socks. He means to avoid scratching and dirtying the platform on which he's working. The platform seems part of the display, not mere scaffold. The designer kneels to attend to a mannequin's shoes, making sure the laces are tied just right. The kneeling appears humble, saintly. The sub-ankle toil recalls the washing of disciple feet. Based on the available evidence, this man in a posture of service has just given his shoes to the mannequin in an act of charity. The double mootness of the sacrifice makes it all the more profound: the mannequin neither understands nor does much walking.

55th and Eighth:

A city is never more city than Friday afternoon at five o'clock and raining. The sidewalks bulge with gray and fidgeting mass. The waiting bodies stand in parallel slanting ranks, glee-club-style. They choose an angle good for spotting buses but not trusting in them.

$A = 0° + $ *(timid anticipation) – (a bus isn't home after all)*

The drizzle, ridiculous next to the week's hurts, gets paid no mind. Around every neck hangs an invisible sign reading, "Soon I'll be who I really am again."

58th and Third:

Sighted: three archetypes in three minutes.

The Sleekness, assiduously groomed, fights to keep character—grace and panache and nostrils pinched with pretense at preoccupation—against the sudden buffeting of startled flapping pigeons.

The Maker, having first heard the Sinatra song in a Tulsa convenience store while microwaving for his girlfriend the sausage rotini entrée from the high-end freezer and who thereafter fetishized Manhattan and visualized himself oh so many times striding sidewalk and showing his cell phone who's alpha, profanities all the while, makes real at this very moment, in front of you and all the passersby, foreign and domestic, his top-of-the-heap fantasy.

The Vincent, an older man, maybe on the brink of loneliness, whose name you do not know to be Vincent but cannot be other than Vincent, wears an overcoat's worth of brushed blanket, green and sumptuous, the hues shifting and mottling as the fabric's tendrils furl and shiver. The coat is obviously expensive, but the cloth tote bag he tucks against his side says the coat is not careless elegance but something actively sought out and saved up for. The shifting and mottling, turns out, are *at* the coat, not *in* the coat: admiration and pity, variously filling and lapping in the observer, as Vincent and his coat are observed.

Tourists:

They fill the sidewalks. They crowd behind, massing and following, their numbers and noise building against the soft blank of your neck. They are the giant boulder in pursuit and you are fresh out of fedoras and bull whips.

They move slow like cattle, of course, and they can't hope to match your grid-forged velocity, and everybody knows you'll outrun them in the end.

None of those reassurances counts for much. They are true of every nightmare.

57th and Seventh:

Even more than the pregnant woman, far more than the old man with a cane, it's the frail elderly woman pushing an empty wheelchair who parts the crowd. She snares minds, tangling them with looping inevitable questions, stunning them with guilt because the questions are cold and ungracious. A wheelchair but she can walk? If it's not for her then for whom? Is her absent companion real or imaginary? You part, too. What else is there to do but part and offer a nodding hello and inadvertently cause her to stop and stare wordlessly?

59th and Fifth:

Every hot dog cart has an extra storage com-
partment that protrudes. Often it's used for buns.
It forms a little shelf at the end of the cart, near
the vendor's left hand. More than once you've
seen a customer, miles from home, eat on that
shelf. For the vendor's part, it is a small hospitality, but also a profit-driven recourse and so no
hospitality at all. It is, therefore, that cardinally
New York thing: at once inherently meaningful
and demonstrably meaningless.

Various:

Nothing rules here except anonymity. Nobody knows anybody. Yet everybody imparts
outsized significance to where nearby strangers
(except tourists near 49th and Fifth, *infra*) are
putting their attention. Look up at a building
and others will look to see what you're looking
at. They're so used to jading and exhaustion that
someone else observing is assurance of something worth observing.

On the other hand, should you be walking
and gazing at your phone, conspicuously failing
to look where you're going, you'll invariably
get run over, bodychecked, shoulder-chickened,
jostled so that your sternum thrums like a xylo-
phone. This is retribution for violating the social
contract that people may be anonymous but not
oblivious.

These scenarios contradict. If attention is so
rare a phenomenon that people are inclined to
follow it wherever it goes, then people shouldn't

resent so prodigiously a failure to pay it.

In this sense New Yorkers are hypocrites. Or enigmas. Or unprincipled opportunists. Or drama engineers who will either find a contretemps by looking or make one by antagonizing. Or blameless stimulus puppets who seek memorable intersection, like the unicellular bacteria that move toward sugar without knowing what it is.

Yeah. That about covers it.

56th and Madison:

People stare into shop windows as they pass. Half view the merchandise inside. These are window shopping. Half view their own reflections, inventorying their own looks. These are window checking. Walking behind, you can tell the window shoppers because their heads are raised a little. They lift their chins and eyes to take in the whole of the window and to pierce beyond its plane and thus throw an arc of gaze that will land a few feet inside. The window checkers look level, a little down. What they want to see is just inches away, and they are scrutinizing for flaw, not admiring with a happy freedom, and so they adopt, without thinking, the assaying posture of the diagnostician, the accuser.

53rd and Sixth:

A motel is a motor hotel. A *molal*, by contrast, is a motor halal.

The *molal* requires a motorist to make passage down a Midtown side street, with or without accompanying passengers. The motorist then approaches a corner where one or more halal street food vendors do business; idles the car, always either *doble parqué* or *en hydrant bloquant*; leaps out as smoothly as circumstances allow; secures the halal; ducks back into the car before detection by traffic police; and, finally, burns through stores of luck by immediately opening the foil pan and eating the contents before bothering to find a creditable parking space.

It is a beautiful thing, the *molal*. The undertaking is mildly illicit, joyful for resembling the graphically pointless fire-drill pranks of frivolous yore, and immensely satisfying for the stark and undeniable reward.

It is, moreover, a kind of redemptive sacrament. Commercial vehicles are part of the city. But leisure driving is very much not. Few Manhattanites own or operate cars. If they do, they generally use them to leave the city. Leisure drivers in Midtown, therefore, mark themselves as members of that disfavored caste: the bridge-and-tunnel type. By performing the sanctifying *molal*, however — by answering that momentous blur of a question: *whitesaucehotsauce?* — they purge away these reductive prejudices and achieve elite insider status, instantly and unimpeachably. No longer are they Jersey brutes, Island oafs, Upstate hicks: they are, to use a term as lurid as that abattoir-floor travesty of the post-*molal* napkin, New Yorkers.

54th and Eighth:

So many celebrities at large you begin to sight the same ones more than once. Depending on where they live, or in what circles they move, you sight them three, four, five times. The sheer repetition degrades the value of having sighted them at all. It persuades you that encountering any particular celebrity is less rare and special than you first believed. It leaves you feeling sheepish for having congratulated yourself on having spotted a celebrity the first couple of times. The pattern eventually antagonizes, because everyone secretly understands themselves to have a fixed allotment of celebrity-sighting luck—an intuitive notion because obviously a person can't expect to run into celebrities every hour on the hour—and these repeat sightings of a now-unspecial celebrity are surely eating into that finite allotment. By making themselves so whorishly available through no fault of their own they force you to resent them and, though galling in the extreme, *they still don't say hi* and, however blameless, still avert their eyes as if they're better than you.

In short, Nathan Lane can go fuck himself.

54th and Lex:

A plume of steam curls from a sewer grate. You recognize it a quarter-block away. Its IMDb filmography is prodigious. Title sequence, *The Equalizer*. Title sequence, *The Jeffersons*. Title sequence, *Night Court*. You head straight for it. You walk through it, you let your calves bathe in it. For two seconds you are not in the city but part of it.

53rd and Seventh:

You've read how New York Ice Cream may have forced Mister Softee from Midtown with a coordinated campaign of harassment, threats, and intimidation. You vow unceasing reprisal. Each time you see a New York Ice Cream truck, you will head straight for it. You will chin-greet the counterman who hangs out the truck's side. You will place the same order:

Double cone one side with chocolate-dipped vanilla and rainbow sprinkles other side with chocolate topped with pineapple chunks and chocolate sprinkles and on the side a cup of crushed cherries and if you need to charge me extra for the crushed cherries that's all right but in that case make it a lot of crushed cherries.

Of all the menu's permutations, it is the order that requires the most assembly.

When finally the attendant leans out to hand over this monstrosity, you will reach, but not close, and say, all excited, "This is Mister Softee, right?!" The attendant at first will not respond, because the question will seem academic, immaterial, and he'll be about the bottom line, intent on delivering the product, but seeing that your query is for whatever reason the thing that is the snag in things he will reply, vexed and dismissive, "No, New York Ice Cream," still thrusting forward in vain.

This is when you will give a little shudder, and produce a little retch, and hold up a sloppy hand, as people do when ineffectually waving off disaster, and walk briskly away.

Mostly this consumer-scale guerrilla tactic will yield tremendous satisfaction. Occasionally it will bring the shadow of regret. When the latter happens, you will think of the Mister Softee song, the sweet-tinkling melody that for decades has wafted from Mister Softee trucks as

they ply sun-washed pavements —

— each note a promise balloon, each note a fore-
shadowing of categorical joy. The delicate piping
is synonymous with felicity itself. The lyrics are
your own. But they are pure truth nonetheless:

Tourists:

They are resented for plural reasons. One,
and not least: they clump together with the same
unnatural density as mammalian herds shield-
ing their smallest and weakest. The visually
striking pattern triggers in locals an urge to play
to role. You see, you attack.

52nd and Eighth:

When you first move to the city, you find an

apartment in the Theater District. The building is lousy with actors. Delroy Lindo, you learn first-hand, is constitutionally incapable of transiting a lobby without echolocating in a vibrato-addled bass. You know that *Cheers* is nonfiction because George Wendt's bustling form does, in fact, stimulate an ungovernable urge to yell "Norm!" Three different residents, one seventy-some-thing and two in their eighties, knock on your door and solemnly advise that you're living in Marilyn Monroe's first apartment in New York. You thank them, thinking only of the hamper built into the bathroom wall. It's original to the apartment. Meaning: your underthings and hers have communed. You are not a coarse individual, but swear to God if anybody living has license to call his penis Mister President.

The morning you're to start your shiny New York job, you dress with obsessive care. You stand at the closet and as you fish out a shirt the closet rod slips out of its wall anchor, dives down like a javelin, and slices with its leading hollow-circle edge the ring toe of your left foot. A half-moon wound there pulses out blood with the melodramatic beat of an arterial gash. The cut gapes and glugs so profusely you're late on your first day of work. You now understand this is how jealous ghosts marry mortals preparing to abandon them: with blood instead of a band, on a foot instead of a hand.

52nd and Park:

Among the confident buildings and the im-possible pace you feel like an amateur. Every-thing around you is institution. You, on the other hand, are miscellaneous, a loose item that's lost its packaging and so can't be explained. You know what you're doing only enough to suppose how you should look while doing it. Also you smell like cough drops.

But consider this taxi. If anything is definitive in this city, it's the yellow cab. Totemic. Ubiquitous. A movie star. Its driver arrived here a month ago. He has few questions, because people have exceedingly few questions when they expect very little.

Consider that doorman. If his fringe-awninged property isn't part of things, you don't know what is. The doorman has seen the doctor and doesn't plan to see the specialist. He doesn't know what he'll do except he'll move to Virginia.

The only institution here is a mistaken presumption that all else is replete and accomplished.

52nd through 49th and Fifth:

A man dressed in a way you recognize from your time in Florida walks down the avenue in Midtown. On his shoulders sits a six-year-old son. The man barks "Good." The boy swings his left hand to his father's face and then takes it away. The boy's holding a cigarette. It's a cigarette he was holding to his father's mouth, and now he's holding it away, in that left hand, to the side and a little behind. The father swivels his head to the right and blows smoke. The father says "Good" again, and several more times, and each time the boy swings his hand in and summons a billow of smoke. Finally the father says

"Done." The boy flicks the butt high in the air — a sky loop — and precisely into the gutter.

Thousands of researchers at work, and yet it's this man who's discovered that the key to relieving secondary smoke of its carcinogenic properties is a simple neck swivel.

50th and Fifth:

A tour guide leads seventy kids and ten grown-ups. This group from middle America — two generations of pale-haired and slow-loping — wears identical T-shirts of first-wear crimson with no design or imagery, only the line "We took a bite out of the Big Apple" and on the back the name of a junior high school.

The tour guide thrusts her hand high above her head as she strides. Her upper arm crushes her ear and her thumb strains for the sky. It's as if she just can't wait to show them something, and has seen fit to drag them all along by an invisible web of wire tied to her exhausted thumb.

She's lost a few. Four or five have fallen behind, clinging to a street corner the rest have trooped past. Pink-skinned, cartoon-eyed, pillow-cheeked. Thirteen years old, maybe. They circle tight, like covered wagons, like sheep when the dogs get loose. They're chanting:

> *New, New, New York City!*
> *Who, Who, Who York City?*
> *Me, Me, Me York City!*
> *You, You, New York City!!!*

Only a third of them say "New York City," there at the end. Pretty sure you're hearing the rest of them screwing up and saying "You York City." Pretty sure this is why so many of them are punitively hitting so many of the others, there at the end.

It's an initiation rite. Young Spartans surely performed similar spectacles on street corners in ancient Athens. Go in force to a rival land, repeatedly abuse its name as loudly as possible before the face of its population, and goad the weakest among you to persist with extravagant shoulder punching.

No, no. It's a decoy unit, to divert attention from the main invasion force. That thumb isn't tired, it's iron, and what she's eager to show them is empire, hers, as far as the eye can see.

Various:

So many people—perfect strangers to each other—take subway seats others have just abandoned, fill food court and restaurant and public plaza seats others have just yielded, settle comfortably in theater seats others have used and left behind, and constantly. Living here means taking turns sitting on the giant egg called New York and hatching the life out of it.

50th through 47th and Sixth:

Sixth Avenue, or Avenue of the Americas, has the Three Sisters. These are three skyscrapers, nearly identical, that loom from the west side of the avenue. They are sere lengths of glass-and-concrete washboard: all three facades consist of long vertical concrete strips alternating with similarly long and slim strips of window.

Each of the buildings has really come into her own. From north to south:

1251 Avenue of the Americas. The tallest, she

has the investment banks, the law firms, a Chase Bank. Also mischief. In December she replaces the fountain out front with a pile of giant red ball-shaped ornaments for the tourists to photograph. Thirteen's bad luck — that's why she lacks a thirteenth floor — and yet every Christmas she puts out thirteen giant ornaments daring people to notice.

1221 Avenue of the Americas. She houses Sirius Radio, both offices and studios — see the celebrities streaming in and out? the graphers stamping and fidgeting at the exits and peering inside? — and a Zibetto Espresso Bar.

1211 Avenue of the Americas: World headquarters for Fox and Fox News.

In sum, a trio very alike and very different: the fun-loving professional, the worldly sophisticate, and the crotchety bigot.

1251, the maven, prefers Sixth Avenue to the fatuous "Avenue of the Americas." It's quicker by five syllables.

1221, the cognoscente, admires "Avenue of the Americas" for its pomp, its sprawl and grandeur.

1211's like, "There's more than one America?"

1211's vertical strips of concrete run about the width of a human body. At ground level, the smokers position themselves unconsciously against the bottom ends of these concrete strips. (Concrete makes for better leaning than glass, and idlers don't especially want to be observed through the windows from inside.) In good weather, so many smokers stand against the concrete strips, and thus array themselves at weirdly uniform intervals, that they look like

a line of infantry who have just fired a volley
with their little smoking muskets. They are so
confident of damage that rather than reloading
they are content to stand idly and gaze across
the battlefield, curious as to whether anything's
survived, convinced more than ever that there's
only one America, goddammit.

49th between Fifth and Sixth:

Men built like boxers, with hydrant arms
and noses like gigged frogs, who sway-walk and
never spit when they talk because growling puts
no premium on the consonants, handle feather
dusters. They use the feather dusters to tickle
their waiting black cars to a polish. They line up
on the cross streets in Midtown and occasionally
stick their heads into each other's windows for a
chat and light cigars and shake out their feather
dusters by banging them in distinctly unmaid-
like fashion against parking meters. If the best
art is dialectic — two unlikes thrust together and
observed in their new context — then a walk
through Midtown during business hours to see
the tough-guy drivers daintying up their cars is
art total and unsurpassed.

Tourists:

Tourists gawk. They crowd a sidewalk, stop
in clumps, and stare at something. New Yorkers
follow a simple rule. They do not look where
the tourists are looking, because they will find
there no blood or nudity. More likely the object
of a tourist's rapture will be some incalculable
wonder like two lights on a pole, or two poles.

New Yorkers disdain tourists, and they do

so for a particular and, moreover, universal reason. It is because early in their New York careers, when they themselves were Floridians or Iowans or even upstate New Yorkers and only freshly arrived to the city, they let themselves be fooled. They'd see a pair of tourists gawking up and they'd gawk too, but there'd be nothing there, or at least nothing of perceptible consequence. They'd see a band of tourists staring across the street and they'd stare too, but their reward was nothing interesting and, moreover, confusion at what it was they thought merited being so urgently observed. They'd look where the tourists looked, and they'd gaze where the tourists gazed, and they'd crane where the tourists craned, and after the ninth or tenth time of being bamboozled of time and effort they decided that they'd had enough and were through being cheated by these saucer-eyed wandering dorks, and — moreover — that if this tribe were so injudicious and provincial as to find fascination in the utterly meritless, and in fact such fascination they were moved to stop and gawk, then it was a tribe with even less to commend it than the negligibles that stopped them in their daft and pitiable tracks.

49th and Fifth:

A man in his fifties wearing yellow glasses drives a silver sedan. He is frozen in traffic. He wants to change lanes to the left. Because this is not Burlington, or Santa Fe, nobody will let him. Then you notice the cigarette.

He is holding one, his arm hanging out of the driver's window. But he is holding it in a way you've never seen anyone hold a cigarette: with five fingers and from above, the way someone holds a knife when cutting a birthday cake. As odd: the ash is long, implausibly and unsustainably long given it suspends itself in the air outside a moving vehicle. His unusual grip and the lopsided ratio between imperiled ash and unburnt stub put you in mind of a spear of some kind or, more precisely, a lance. His disheveled hair forms a kind of ruff on the top of his skull above the glasses. Of course: the knight's visor, the horsehair-crest. You also notice his mouth is open, he is breathing through his mouth, as if exercised, and — given that he is seated comfortably in a modern sedan — you infer he is a heavy smoker with bad sinuses and possible respiratory issues and a compensating inclination to mouth-breathe. Instantly you are put in mind of the precedent for breathing hard notwithstanding a seated position: the warrior on a horse; the knight on a steed.

Of course he's changing lanes to the left. Don't all jousting knights tend left — toward the enemy, along the vector needing maximum force?

Foe finally yields — traffic moves — and he rides away.

49th and Third:

New York steak houses cheat with butter. They butter the skillet in which they cook the steak, and the steak while it's cooking, and the steak again as it's plated. They use so much butter they smell more like bakeries than steak houses. If starving Neanderthals were transport-

ed to a steak house in present-day Manhattan
through the space-time wormhole that is located
at the foot of the Rockefeller Plaza flagpole bearing the Botswanan flag, they would walk right
by, like zombies past a scarecrow, because they
wouldn't recognize the weird superheated-dairy
odor as that of cooking meat.

48th and Sixth:
    Crossing to the intersection's southeast cor-
ner, you see an altercation. No. You hear it before you see it: two counterfeit purse vendors.
    The taller of the two paces the corner and
shouts things like, "I'll kill you" and "Come over
here and you'll see, I'll kill you" and "I'll kill
you." The shorter of the two has launched west
across the avenue, putting distance between him
and his counterpart. But he's turned half around
as he walks, and each time Tall shouts something, Short calls out, "Pap-pap-pap-pap-pap-
pap" in what sounds like a naturally high voice,
but made blaring and plangent for mockery's
sake. Each time Tall stops talking, Short stops
papping. Each time Tall lofts another threat or
insult, Short re-paps.
    Short has won. It's not because of gross
optics, obviously. With the sound turned off,
Tall appears the victor: his rival flees while his
ground is stood. It's the auditory record that
clinches Short's triumph. Tall has let his voice
creep higher and higher with rage and agitation,
has ceded his sturdiness, has yielded to the juve-
nile and high-pitched influence of his adversary.
Has, finally, turned papper himself.

47th and Sixth:

The shoe shiner has uranium-235–grade energy, a fondness for calling out to prospective customers, and a talent for deriding the state of their shoes. This is his marketing campaign of twenty years. Half-life fuel means he'll be doing it for two hundred more. His default patter is a two-liner, recited as he fixes the passerby's shoes with a scandalized look: "YOU TRYING TO GET AHEAD?! YOU THINK THEY WON'T NOTICE?!"

Brilliant lines, brilliantly delivered. They are questions, not statements, and one can't be resented for merely asking questions. They lock onto the insecurities of young professionals and burrow with prejudice under their pink, anxiety-sodden meninges. Effortlessly they link something as small as shined shoes with things as large as career and identity. They are bellowed so the whole block can hear. The scandalized look blossoms into a hot, bulge-eyed, disbelieving stare.

He has put two kids through college.

Tourists:

Tourist season begins March 17, Saint Patrick's Day. The date is apropos. Patrick expelled from Ireland a plague of snakes, and God will not undo that feat. But He will enforce the natural laws, including that of trade-offs, and so the blessing is paid with a curse: a different kind of pest, visited on the place with the most Irish on Earth, and on Saint Patrick's own day.

Tourist season ends the Sunday of the first full weekend after New Year's Day. If January

1 falls on a Friday, for example, it ends the Sunday two days later, but if January 1 is Saturday it ends eight days later on the following Sunday. The shifting date has to do with recovery time and travel plans. The variability is apropos. The tourist is a recalcitrant thing: easy to attract, hard to repel. Asked when tourist season ends, a New Yorker's answer must be as qualified and complicated as the exterminator's, asked when the roaches finally will go away.

The tween season, between New Year's Sunday and St. Patrick's? For the young, those dates are gate posts to a cold, forbidden territory. Between them stretches nothing but gray and joyless desolation.

For the old, just the opposite. It's when New York opens its petals. The pests are gone, the young stay home and masturbate indifferently and think about the beach. The museums are quiet and navigable, the restaurants are festive but not teeming. The city is finally theirs. Adult swim. New York's gift to the aging.

Between revelry and revelry: reverie.

47th and Sixth:

You see your first dog stroller. The U-235 shoeshiner sees it too. It breaks his brain. It happens when two women walk behind him as he bends to his work. One woman carries a dog, the other pushes an empty stroller. The stroller is a creepy, parallel-dimension version of a baby stroller: half the width and covered at front and top with a zippered netting.

The shoeshiner looks idly, notices, looks back again, computes what's happening, gives a great

heaving start that begins with his eyes and trav-
els downward, and finally gives up his work—
dropping his hands to his sides and taking a
great step back—to get a better look. Still with
his hands at his sides, his abdomen distending
like what's coming is an involuntary expulsion,
he peals out, "AND YOU CARRYING HIM?!"

The women turn around, one says something and laughs, he stares and stares, what
they say is of no moment, his abdomen shifts
and works again. "HE SHOULD BE PUSHING
YOU!!" Nothing they say can mend his broken
brain. "*HE* SHOULD BE PUSHING *YOU!!*"

48th and Madison:

A wave rises where the eastern edge of the
avenue meets the curb. Better put, the road
pavement forms the shape of a wave—an ocean
wave, two feet across, peaking and curling just
as a wave should, but made of tar and asphalt.
It rears there, frozen in time, always daring
and risking and never crashing. Someone from
Laborers' Local 1010 took a Winston break
during the resurfacing job and forgot to finish.
Its effect on the surroundings is outsized. The
street becomes ocean, the sidewalk turns to
shore. Pedestrians are still pedestrians, but beach-
going now, loosed from harness and wandering
the waterfront.

The wave rises two-thirds of a block north
of Grand Central's back entrance. The commuters throng this part of shore at the same sighing
time of day that, at the real shore, brings out the
beachcombers, the powerwalkers, the resort bar
hoppers.

The wave surges eastward, which means the sun will set over the other side of the street, which means you'll be able to teeter on the curb, hand over eyes, and see mournfulness and hopefulness in the same sky.

Various:

At the turn of the (current) century, Times Square had a hundred stores that sold the same inventory: tourist-nip. They sold T-shirts, coffee mugs, snow globes, travel mugs, sunglasses that if they could talk would be heard to mutter "UV protection? What's UV protection?," mugger hats with sports team logos and/or the word *Sexy* in a lascivious cursive, coasters, refrigerator magnets, sweatpants with text printed across the ass (again, *Sexy*, scrawled always in 156-point Languid Debasement), hot-dog-shaped wallets, poster-sized caricatures of random celebrities backgrounded by random New York landmarks (the saddest inventory of all, for the implication that the featured celebrities had come in person to have their caricatures hand-drawn in real time by resident caricaturists taking an artist's sabbatical from their sidewalk busking, with the impossibility of the prospect making it exactly as pathetic as fatuous), and keychains.

These stores, with different owners, nonetheless all bore the same name: "Cameras Computers Gifts Luggage." The name was also a bluff inventory, cannily proposing that anything that was not a camera, a computer, or a piece of luggage was—must be—a gift. The name's disdain for commas and conjunctions telegraphed a breathlessness, an irrepressible, glee-filled excitement that hoped to be contagious.

Today, these stores are endangered. Only half remain. Even the name is half what it was: "Gifts Luggage." No cameras: smartphones mean nobody buys them. No computers: on-line commerce and brand-operated retail make selling them impossible. The stores have revised the name for relevance and remain tenaciously in business. You know they will continue to do so, they will do whatever they need to survive, because you know the truth. The Gifts Luggage stores are tourist hatcheries. They are where the masses of brightly clad, brightly chattering strangers come from. It's no coincidence that the suitcases and roller boards and shoulder bags are lined up in size sequence. This is how you keep hatcheries in good order. Out of these and onto the sidewalks of Manhattan will wriggle full-grown tourists, proceeding glacially as they acclimate to a gray new world, legs awobble, newt-tender eyes still sensitive to light, open mouths working as if to beg nourishment and betray adorable confusion at how it could be that, no matter where and how far they roam, the right way to the subway is always down.

47th between Sixth and Fifth:

Jewelry Row is a scrum. The street chokes with undecided fiancés and double-parked oligarchs. The sidewalks teem with shop barkers and window gazers and Bukharan meat-and-three pamphleteers.

Then comes the first Wednesday after Thanksgiving. A weird calm falls. The Rockefeller

Christmas tree gets its lights. The massive stalk of bling on 49th upstages the little trays of bling on 47th. The crowds shift two blocks north. Jewelry Row empties, turns severe with dusky space. The street becomes a sorry wind-whisked pavement and the sidewalks amount to an afterthought. It's precisely the time of year when people shop en masse for giftable objects. Jewelry Row should be humming with bodies and purpose, not hollowed out.

But stones can't compete with a bush on fire. Even God knows this. It's why He entrusted Moses with two of the former only after grabbing his attention with the latter.

47th and Fifth:

There are three buildings of which Greeks everywhere are most proud. First, the Parthenon. Second, the Temple to Zeus. Third, the Greek-owned building on the corner of Fifth and 47th. It's the one that flies a Greek flag and anchors the eastern end of Jewelry Row, the famous redoubt of Jews with loupes. It is a matter of ethnic pride that Greeks might be one-upping the only others they respect as anywhere close to the same league of business savvy, and *in their own territory.* More than once your Greek father has told you how Greeks admire and observe what may or may not be, but what Greeks nonetheless call, the Jewish Rule.

Jews will help a Jew twice.

But if he fails twice, then the third time they will not help him.

Because then he is not a Jew, he is a worthless bastard.

You tell your father it's the kind of line that surely Homer, in his grave, profoundly regrets not having woven into his verse. Your father shrugs and gives a quick grimace. Which, translated from the Greek, means, Well, this Homer's got one more chance, doesn't he?

46th and Sixth:

The first Chik-fil-A in New York opened here a few years ago. This happened for the same reason that fires eat forests. It restored balance. It put things aright. Crowds of New Yorkers, manically delighted by this exotic import from the South, still line up outside at meal times. They throng for food the rest of the nation likes well enough but basically takes for granted. Thus it affords tourists, that long abused and relentlessly derided minority, an opportunity to reassert their dignity and sovereignty. Now the tourists get to shake their heads at the locals for their acute and conspicuous hypocrisy, for doing precisely all the things New Yorkers are constantly defaming tourists for doing: standing in lines; taking up valuable sidewalk space; acting in mindless droves; eating at chain restaurants; doing these things in improvident lieu of New York–unique experiences. Like the slicing of Marie Antoinette's neck, the proton torpedoing of the Death Star, the rousting of fugitive dictators from holes: a Chik-fil-A in New York is the underclass's definitive vengeance.

46th between Fifth and Sixth:

Just inside every loading dock in the world is the worst an indoor space can be while still being indoors and, thus, deliberate in some sense. Invariably it is a dim, lurking, low-ceilinged squalor, one that relies for alibi on its utilitarian purpose. Let us call this kind of superlatively grim space an *omega space*. Auxiliary mine shafts, ordnance-decommissioning diving bells, and dungeons: these are omega spaces. So is Kosher Deluxe. Of all the city's omega spaces, it is maybe the ugliest that is meant to house a paying clientele.

Yet it is a felicitous space, lucky and implausible. A higher seat-to-sitter ratio than any coffee shop or public plaza. A greater indifference than even the public library's to how long you stay and what you do, with crepuscular lighting as a kind of guarantee against scrutiny. Where else are you so genuinely and entirely left alone? You've got it wrong. It's not an omega space. It's a feral space, a rare piece of urban wild. The ugliness is so formidable that it is a kind of perverse certificate of worth, like the neurosurgeon's rudeness or the diva's farting.

Kosher Deluxe boasts two counters: a shawarma counter along the side and a main food counter across the back. The massive menu behind the main counter runs the breadth of the back wall, with Chinese food on the left, breakfast options on the right, and sandwiches and salads and fast food in the middle. The single most interesting item is the "Sino Steak Sandwich Club." It's been years since you last encountered *Sino* as a term for things Chinese. Also it's a "Sandwich Club," not a "Club Sandwich," so with every purchase you get membership in a sandwich society, apparently, or a subscription to sandwiches. This is the kind of development that bears on status and identity. You should have worn cologne this morning.

At the back counter stands an older man, calm and authoritative. He puts so much of his hands and forearms on the counter that maybe he wants to be part of the counter. You ask him what *Sino* means. As always with this kind of journalistic meta-query, it takes several presidential administrations for you to make clear to him what you're talking about. Finally, he nods.

"It's tenderloin."

"As opposed to?"

"It's tenderloin. It's more tenderized."

"How do you tenderize it?"

"The meat is nice. We make it more tender."

"What's the regular steak sandwich made of?"

"The steak sandwich is just meat. The Sino is more tender because we tenderize it. It's more tenderized."

"How do you make it more tender?"

"Tenderize. We tenderize it."

The times you wish a member of your family were a contractor or a plumber or a sorcerer are many. This is the rare occasion you wish for a molecular chemist. You'd bet the price difference between a Sino Steak Sandwich Club and a Steak Sandwich Club that there is no other difference between a Sino Steak Sandwich Club and a Steak Sandwich Club.

Which, to be clear, is not a little money.

Tourists:

One thing you'll say for them: they smell good. If you're in the mood for a sweet scent, you know you can just trawl past the dense lines outside NBC Studios or Ellen's Stardust Diner and snuffle up the airborne nectar. There's more than one reason they're so fragrant. Their hotel rooms bristle with complimentary scented hair and skin products. The rooms are often chosen for proximity and remain available throughout the day without interference from workplace obligation, and so freshening is frequent. Most important, these people are on *vacation* — every block is a destination, every activity an event, every experience a drama for recounting to friends at home — and so ablutions and ministrations are anticipation-grade.

Finally, let's not forget: they're not all bad. Some, in fact, are ethical types, decent and upstanding. Some understand they should smell good to compensate for all their bullshit.

45th and Broadway:

The panhandlers who claim affiliation with larger organizations are the boldest, the loudest. They call to individuals in the passing crowd. They address the females as "ma'am" and "young lady," the males as "big guy" and "young man." The loudhandlers carry a Punnett square in their heads and think they know what everybody wants:

	FEMALE	MALE
YOUTH	regard	power
AGING	youth	youth

So they think they know what everybody wants to hear:

	FEMALE	MALE
YOUTH	regard "ma'am"	power "big guy"
AGING	youth "young lady"	youth "young man"

The loudhandlers ingratiate themselves by first validating and then appeasing our deepest desires. Only once the mark is thus primed comes the ask: You in a giving mood today, big guy? You got room in your heart, young lady?

New Yorkers, for their part, can isolate with precision the date and time of that pivot of pivots: when they have ceased being young. It comes the first time a loudhandler calls them "young lady" or "young man."

It's happened to you already. You don't remember the year. You remember it happened in August. Of course it did. August is the season of things going a little to rot. The gold in the light yields to red — that past-tense color, testimony to what's happened, the wound and the bloom and the words that shame — and even the night turns flabby with warmth.

45th and Lex:

The greediest thing you've ever seen is a middle-aged man open a fortune cookie, read his fortune, and then thumb the edge of the paper, vainly and repeatedly, to see if it would unfold and yield him still more.

You have a friend who says a fortune comes true only if the cookie's eaten. You have a second friend who takes this further and spits out the cookie if the fortune is not to his taste.

A third friend loves fortune cookies but spits them out every time, regardless of the fortune. She believes there is no fate but what she wills.

This third friend does not exist. It is the person you wish you were, you try to be, but something — fate? lack of will? isn't the first what we call the second? — gets in the way.

0th and Never:

One thing you've never seen but would like to see — the kind of thing that is as unlikely to happen as the prospect of its never happening seems implausible — is someone fanning themself with a pizza slice. Just once.

44th and Lex:

This corner houses a world-class law firm. Your sister once worked there. She joined the firm out of law school to work in its elite tax department. Her first day was a class-wide orientation. All the incoming lawyers — some of the country's brightest young legal minds — assembled in a large conference room. At the podium in front, senior partners and other key personnel took turns addressing life and work at the firm. At breaks, the attendees roved to the tables at the sides and rear of the room and sampled the snacks and cookies and coffee.

Late that morning, during an especially long and monotonous session, a young man rose from his seat, took a step, and stopped. Nobody thought anything of it. Perhaps he had to go to the restroom. Except he wasn't going anywhere. He was staring, and his face was strange, and he was making noises like he wasn't getting air, and now he was shaking. He was having a seizure. One of the other new attorneys, seeing he was in distress, yelled, "Somebody get him a cookie!" Nobody got him a cookie. The young man was suffering an epileptic fit. Others understood this. A person who knew him from law school got up and took him by the arm and helped him outside the room. The young man received medical attention and soon was all right. He came to work the next day and was just fine. He had no memory of being offered a cookie, or of anyone intrepidly instructing others to feed him a cookie.

He was the only one. Everybody else in the room remembered. And they wondered: Get him a cookie? The implications were troubling. Get him a cookie, the way a tantrumming child is appeased? The way a vicious dog is tossed a treat?

In fairness, the new attorney who proposed the cookie thought it might be diabetes. The new attorney had learned somewhere, maybe from *Parade* magazine, or an episode of *Mr. Belvedere,* that an intake of sugar can save a diabetic in distress. The new attorney was your sister, of course. She saw the cookies on the table and put two and two together.

You love your sister. She is smarter than you. But we all blow it in the extreme from time to time. And little brothers exist for the purpose of remembering those moments and recounting them endlessly and fiendishly. Hence you recount all this because you must. Hence you will also tell how this is the same sister who just a few months later would phone the Florida Bar; advise that she'd just passed the New York Bar Examination, widely considered the country's toughest; and ask with great dispatch what the fees and application requirements were and what reciprocity if any existed between the Florida and New York Bars.

Whereupon the man on the other end of the line would reply, "Ma'am, this is a tavern?"

Various:

The deli is the quintessential example of a prism thing. The prism thing shows uniform or homogenous to the naif, the outsider. For the discerning adept, however, it contains such strikingly various subtypes that the unitary name is strictly expedient and barely coherent. There is, for example, the kind of deli that mutes the home-and-garden programming on its wall-mounted television and plays music that puts you in mind of dirt flying off spinning tires, so that together these result in the most ironic and least accountable music videos imaginable. There is the kind of deli that is more a lottery counter than anything else and the kind of deli that is more a grill than anything else and the kind of deli that is more a hot bar than anything else. There is the low-end deli with an enclosed cooler, looking like the pantry in a widow's Queens apartment; the middle-class deli with a wall of enclosed coolers, aspiring to be a supermarket; the premium deli with a wall of open-face coolers, affecting with its aggressive climate projection to be the mall.

Tourists:

People eating reveal their circumstances by the shape of their bites.

Those at leisure take bites like bowls. Their mouths are full, like they're ready to pronounce *o*'s and *u*'s.

Those under stress take bites like disks. Their mouths stay prim and disapproving because efficiency looks prim and impatience disapproving. These mouths are poised for faster and shallower vowel action: *e*'s and *i*'s.

You can see both these ends of the bite spectrum when you pass through a Midtown hotel restaurant in summer. The pods of vacationers laze in the moment and bowl-bite. The squads of business-trippers disk-bite and sweat bitter anticipatory sweat and continually refocus after losing focus because they're eating, but eating— something so small as eating, as living, surviving—cannot be the focus.

43rd and Eighth:

It is very much a Midtown thing to dispose of very small things in very large things. You flick a piece of lint into a waist-high barrel. You toss a gum wrapper into a neck-high dumpster. It's consolation. You're so obviously dwarfed by the city—rattling around inside it in antic patterns resembling aimlessness—that it's comforting to see your personal detritus still more obviously dwarfed. You're not alone.

42nd and Sixth:

Avoid intrusions into others' personal space. It's a basic rule of human behavior. Here it counts as iron law. Except for the little grinning monks. Their flouting is conspicuous. They make saffron beelines for the nearest intelligence, then reach their hands still closer to pass off a bit of paper printed with an aphorism or a donation request. It's their frank straight-line vectors that are most startling, even more unsettling than the ultimate moment of encounter. By charging straight for you they trigger a whole matrix of evolution-coded autonomic antipredatory instincts. Their gait, also, is curious. Not so much the straight spines—we'd expect no less from a monk—but the waistlines forward like they have a secret they can't wait to share, and the feet skimming the ground like they don't want to wake anybody as they share it. The Midtown monks are the world's worst panhandlers or the best, depending on whether their aim is to coax rapport or to stoke apprehension. Bright smiles and meek feet suggest one, provocative bellies and headlong trajectories the other. Avoid intrusions into other minds with irreconcilable contradictions? They flout that rule, too.

Various:

The buildings have three kinds of canopies extending from door to curb. The first kind is what newer apartment buildings wear. It perches at a modest angle: between one and fifteen degrees from horizontal.

It resembles an idle skateboard on the ground, lightly toed. The mild incline is to reassure those

passing underneath that, far from sagging and
threatening to fall, the canopy up-prongs with a
surfeit of structural integrity — like a stone ramp,
or a boulevard to better things. This kind of canopy is like the Parthenon's deformed columns,
built deliberately thicker in the middle than at
the ends. The thing is made irregular so that it
can look regular.

The second kind is worn by hotels. It elevates
more markedly, at between fifteen and thirty
degrees.

This suggests an aimed cannon, offering to
point and launch the observer into the surround-
ing city. "Have no fear of missing out," this
canopy announces. "Stay here and we'll make
sure you're where you need to be."

The third kind, favored by marketing-driven
merchantry, cants at a ludicrous angle of forty or
forty-five degrees.

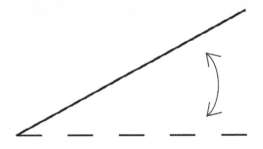

The diagonal jut suggests a flag. This, in turn, signals pride and sovereignty, announces that for which it stands, and thus maximizes attention to itself. It cares about exactly that: itself, not at all about the human noticing it, except to the extent the human notices it.

42nd and Vanderbilt:

Pick one experience as quintessential New York. Easy. It's standing in the middle of Grand Central's Great Hall and gazing up at the ceiling. The choice is plain. New York is a city of interiors — more or less an elegantly dense cubic mass of structure — and the Great Hall is probably its best. New York is Gotham, a city of noir, and the ceiling in question depicts the night sky. New York is a city of crowd and peril, the capital of momentous happenstance, and as you gawk upward you're not only not looking where you're not going but also exposing to the heedless buffeting throngs the most vulnerable part of you: a tender length of carotid-fronded windpipe.

(Also, standing and staring is a way of telling those you are inevitably obstructing, who for their part are mostly taking the trouble to look where they're going, to fuck off, and New York is also the capital of fuck off.)

37th and Park:

The slow saunter down the fat middle of a sidewalk, dismissive of the possibility that others behind might favor the normal pace of a bipedal hominid, is called a coronation walk. An inordinate number of men in their thirties and forties wearing suits in Midtown do the coronation walk. Also in their twenties and fifties. You can't move without encountering every few feet whole drifts of men looking intently down at their phones while lolling. They resemble landing parties from the *USS Enterprise,* peering down at their tricorders as they trammel through alien territory with unfounded conviction. You have half a mind to pap at them. Instead you find solace in two facts. First, the *Star Trek* Law of Landing Parties dictates that persons who are Spock survive every foray and persons who are not Spock routinely die. Second, and critically, none of these indifferent and discourteous men has pointy ears.

Tourists:

On rare occasion, when circumstances align — the tourists on a particular piece of sidewalk outnumber the locals, the ambient fracas builds and maintains, a pair of busker acrobats bark warmly at a captivated crowd the very moment a brisk passerby sheathed in next-season outerwear barks punitively into his Bluetooth — the world wobbles in its frame and you look about and suddenly you are made to understand you are not in a city but in a massive interactive performance, and you, hailing from just a few blocks away, are part of the show and must stop immediately what you're doing, which is goggling about you, open-mouthed and overmastered, like a kindergarten teacher freshly stumbled onto an orgy, because you are singlehandedly endangering the authenticity of the scene, by seeming weak, seeming passive.

This, of course, is *the one thing* New York–based cast members don't do.

35th and Third:

A standpipe says who they are. Do they use it for sitting and catching their breath when they've just come out of the clinic? Do they prop a foot to refasten their available-only-in-Hong-Kong SuperMaxAir Halospheres? Do they lean bags so they can straighten their infant daughter's hat so that it's a hat again, not an eyepatch? Do they use it to pretend to look for something because here comes the love of their life, known to everyone as their ex, because they Jewish- ruled themselves out of the best thing they ever knew?

40th and Eighth:

Gray's Papaya is Midtown's resort. Its signature juices are from the tropics. These have nothing to do with New York. Its ethic of friendliness—in the signage, in the color scheme, in the counterstaff—is from the tropics. This has nothing to do with New York. You have a friend visiting from out of town. You turn to her and say, "Let's go to the beach." On the way you pass the wave at 48th and Madison (*supra*) and when she points you gently shake your head no. Finally, you arrive. "A hot dog place?" she asks.

Let her review the evidence.

The flavors: beach.

GRAY'S	BEACH
meat	cookout
salt	seawater
sweet	fruit
smoke	bonfire
tang	sex

The stand-only eating: beach.

GRAY'S	BEACH
No seats. Only that skinny counter that rings the place and faces the windows. Keep behind you the hissing grill and the gurgling juice vats and the wheezing, jangling register. Watch in front of you the flowing masses of people.	Behind you buzzes civilization, hot and complicated. In front heaves a whole living realm, apart and infinite.

Why always served painfully hot off the grill? Why coconut champagne, of all things?

Scorching hot sand. Check. Suntan lotion. Check.

42nd and Fifth:

There are times you feel slight and forgettable. Also futile: every time you inhale, you just end up exhaling. When this mood finds you, you go to the corner of Fifth and 42nd. If it's morning, you walk east, toward Grand Central. If it's afternoon, or evening, you walk away from Grand Central. This way, no matter the time, you tend against the commuting masses. The mob surges one way, you go opposite. Your progress forces oncomers to pause and dodge. They pay tribute with head bobs, body bladings, side skitters, course resets.

Ha, someone might think. These accommodations are reflexive, negligible. They mean nothing. No matter how numerously and successively accumulated, there is no power in them.

Ha, you think about someone's thinking. Really? Why wake each morning to split the air? Why speak, sweat, love? Death is the mob. On-coming, oncoming, the end of all things we know in pitiless pieces. At least make it go around. Life is a series of insistences that it at least go around.

Tourists:

Tourist's Guide to Midtown Manhattan, Section 3 ("Capturing the Experience Forever: Photos and Videos"):

> "Midtown is where you go to ask passing strangers to take your photo and get de-clined for the first time in your life."

Local's Guide to Midtown Manhattan, Section 5 ("Tourists and the Pain They Make in Your Ass"):

> "When asked, don't just push away the phone or camera. Deliver a line they can take back home with them— perhaps we owe them that much—and don't break stride as you do. Examples:
> - 'The judge said I couldn't.'
> - 'You are beautiful, you don't need proof.' [Said, obviously, as if not exactly meant.]
> - 'You don't understand. If you send me a copy I'll get sad, and if you don't send me a copy I'll get mad, really really really mad. Like, *really* mad.'"

39th and Fifth:

You have a favorite among the hometown department stores. You pick one on the same es-sentially arbitrary basis a four-year-old chooses a Green Bay Packers–themed bedspread: for the pleasure of felt affiliation, for a way of converting ambient enthusiasm about a larger pursuit (whether football or full-floor retail) into actionable kinship. It is Lord and Taylor. L&T is your team. The flagship store broadcasts the National Anthem over the intercom each morning at opening. They hang rows and rows of chandeliers from the ceiling, invite climbing fantasies just plausible enough that the temptation isn't mockery. On summer days, walking by, you duck through the main doors, weave through the cosmetics counters, and breathe the cold perfumed air with heady pleasure. At the back wall you turn right. There, just around the corner of the wall that divides the elevator bank from the shopping floor you've just transited, waits the water cooler with the paper cones. You drink a cone. You drink three or four. Thus refreshed, looked after, you walk out again.

Occasionally you buy something. You're not a total leech. Your favorite scarf is from the L&T flagship. It is the rare item you plucked not from some clearance rack in a perimeter hinterland but from the good table, the one out in the open with full-price, early-season items folded and nestled successively in rows, like bodies at a bus stop on a Friday afternoon.

The store announces it will close. Permanently. You visit a last time, during the final liquidation sale. This is a mistake. Someone has ripped away the elegance, leaving only desperation splatched with adhesive residue. Vitrines holding fragrance bottles wear hand-lettered sheets of paper taped onto their glass fronts. It's as if L&T is trying for inelegance, a final bid at conspicuous baseness to atone for all the decades of profit-mandated pretense in the opposite direction. You scrutinize the signs to see how deeply they've discounted the fragrances and learn nothing. The signs quote prices for the glass cases themselves. The final sale is so total — tables, mirrors, waist-down-only mannequins — it's hard to tell what's for sale and what's not. A street-legal motor scooter lies on its side on the tenth floor between a scuffed floor lamp with a tag and a shiny floor lamp without. Which of these three is for sale? If you stand still long enough, are *you* for sale?

Having returned to the first floor, you don't need to look. You already know it's gone. It was the first thing you checked when you walked in. You went straight back and turned right and saw it wasn't there. The water cooler hadn't survived long enough to get a sign.

Life is a progressive loss of things that let us feel looked after. Teachers, friends, lovers, parents, certainty, a winning record, a dependable constitution, a presumption that absent everything else there at least reigns an overall benign logic, a sense of intactness. You walk out a last time.

Tourists:

There is something iconic about the out-of-state mom who goes abroad in the city with a rabble of un-kin teens — the soccer team, the debate club, the ad hoc spring-break crew. TourMom is sweaty and disoriented but game. Circumstances conspire to cow her but she shows bluster to compensate. TourMom keeps either very close focus (to stay immersed in the familiar) or very far focus (to figure out where she's going or what she's missing) but never medium focus (to avoid gratuitous entanglement with the locals). She maintains an excellent upright posture that wants to sag but is not let to. TourMom swings often from strident cheer to ritualized puzzlement. She is a Platonic form for *Best-under-the-circumstances,* a metaphor for all-purpose *We-shall-triumph-and-let-me-worry-about-how* deployment. At 4:45 p.m. on April 15 in line at the post office you grip your tax return envelope with perspiring fingers that leave escargot-pan depressions: you're Tour-Mom. The doctor's office asks, presumably for a reason, if you have any other kind of insurance: you're TourMom. TourMom exists so that, having her example, the rest of us may fail more nobly.

39th and Broadway:

Your mother tells the story of how, freshly arrived in Manhattan, she momentarily lost her way. She tried to orient herself, but as she took in her surroundings she only got more confused. Finally she asked an older woman passing by:

"Where's Fifth Avenue?"

Without hesitating, without looking where she was pointing — indeed, without looking at your mother — the woman hooked a thumb over her shoulder and, as she continued on her way, replied, "It was there this morning."

When you were eight, and ten, and, if we're being honest, every fifth hour of that part of life wherein both of two conditions obtained — you lived in the same house as your mother and you had the power of speech — you'd ask your mother where something was. She'd reply along the lines of: "It's probably where you left it."

Midtown, like life, is brute and teacher.

34th and Eighth:

The Garment District is your favorite. The first stories brightly beckon but their windows show inventories so particular and recondite — bandings, cordings, charmeuses, gazars, dupionis, korhogos, D-rings, mudcloths, ultrasuedes, and, obviously, lampworked Czech beads — that you can't envision a circumstance where you'd have anything to do with them. The higher stories brood darkly. They can't be bothered to tell what they're up to. The ubiquity of secrets here is so weird your throat feels hot. You've never encountered a place where there is simultaneously so much mystery and so much noise. Sound reveals, just like observation, but though the boom and shriek and scritch and clatter are prodigious, you don't know a thing about what's making them.

34th and 6th:

A window at Macy's shows a window designer, live, fixing the inseam of a mannequin's suit pants at the crotch. A young thin-haired man on the sidewalk stops to watch.

After a few moments he loses patience. He hand-bangs the window, palm convex and fingertips splayed, over and over. He favors the inside part of the hand, so it's his thumb and his index finger and the webby half-moon between them that repeatedly hits the glass. Over and over he smacks this capital-C shape against the window and yells, "That's not nice! That's not nice!"

Is he joking? No. You're behind him and to the side. You can tell he's not joking. So can the designer, which is why she's working so calmly it's obvious she's in a panic.

"That's not nice!" He's still yelling and smacking. He's a yell-and-smack machine.

The designer eyes him once, then, eyeing him again, decides finally on a new approach. She steps around and pretends to straighten out a wall dressing made to look like a parchment map. This placates him enough for quiet. But he's eyeing her just the same, his whole body pricked up with indignant purpose. It's clear she has nothing left to do, except to wait for him to leave. It's equally clear he's not going anywhere so long as she's in harassing distance of his mannequin friend. It's a standoff.

But now *you* have to leave. Macy's doesn't pay your salary, and this mannequin has not once invited you to a party. As you walk away, ruefully, you wonder so many questions — "Who was that young man?" "What did he think she was doing?" "What place did the map show?" "What's the C stand for?" — that it doesn't even occur to you to wonder, not until the next block, when or how it ends, or whether one can assume it ends, and if they might still be there even now, the two of them, caught forever in the amber of view-warbling shopwindow glass, in the silt of the city's pooty air.

ACKNOWLEDGMENTS

"Paylessness," *Chattahoochee Review* XXXX, no. 1
        (Spring 2020): 95–106. Finalist, 2020 Lamar
        York Prize for Nonfiction.

"Why I Write," *Fiction Southeast,* April 16, 2018.

"Why I Write," republished in *Little Stories Big Ideas,*
        April 16, 2018, Best Flash Fiction Online.

"I [Hard-Clenched Knuckle-Forward Fist] New York,"
        Confrontation, no. 119 (Spring 2016): 172–75.

"I [Hard-Clenched Knuckle-Forward Fist] New York,"
republished in *Broad Street* (Summer/Fall 2019).

"The Vengeances," *Harvard Review*, no. 48 (2016):
        174–88.

"87th and Abomination," *World Literature Today*
        (Winter 2021): 42–43.

"The Petervian Calendar," previously published as
        "Fun with Peter," *Post Road*, no. 36 (Spring
        2020): 131–32.

"Dead Now," *Boulevard* 32, no. 1 (Fall 2016): 75–80.

"Tampa, Florida, 1184 B.C.," *Gargoyle* 28 (2016): 28–30.

"Glory, Finally, at the Parker House," *Arts & Letters,* Issue 38 (Spring 2019): 94–101.

"Nothing Like a Pandemic," *Broad Street* (April 9, 2020).

"My Muse Is Gaffay," *Passages North Online*, no. 96 (December 1, 2014).

"In the Covidium," *New World Writing,* July 27, 2020.

ABOUT THE AUTHOR

GEORGE CHOUNDAS's award-winning writing has appeared in over seventy-five publications. His story collection, *The Making Sense of Things (FC2)*, won the Ronald Sukenick Innovative Fiction Prize and was shortlisted for the Robert C. Jones Prize for Short Prose, the St. Lawrence Book Award for Fiction, and the Katherine Anne Porter Prize in Short Fiction. His mother, born in Cuba, was a flyer at Macy's Manhattan flagship until she saved enough to travel Europe for a year. His father, born in Greece, was a tanker captain who, aboard a passenger ship transporting him to his next command, met an engaging American tourist with a Cuban accent. Choundas is a former FBI agent who worked against public corruption in the Bureau's New York Office. He lives with his family in Pleasantville, New York.

Explore more nonfiction published by

EASTOVER
—— PRESS ——

Hidden Cargoes
Chris Arthur

"One of our greatest living essayists, Chris Arthur brings
a rare combination of tenderness, power, care and,
at times, ghoulish humor to the page." — PHILLIP LOPATE

ᖆᕽᘿ

Homesick for Nowhere
Richard LeBlond

A witty and informative collection of stories about travel, the
natural world, and life over eighty pondered by a retired field
biologist with an acutely-tuned eye and ear for observation.

ᖆᕽᘿ

More or Less: Essays from a Year of No Buying
Susannah Q. Pratt

"These essays will give you new ways of thinking
and talking about consumerism and late capitalism.
Each essay is engaging and beautiful." — ANDREW ROOT

ᖆᕽᘿ

The Cutleaf Reader

Our annual print anthologies collect works by numerous
established and emerging writers as published in *Cutleaf*,
our literary journal of short stories, essays, and poetry.
(www.CutleafJournal.com)